"Every parent knows that kids ask questions. And as the kids get older, the questions become increasingly important. Jim Johnson and Paul Basden give specific, real-world answers that really work. They have a way of making us smile while talking about some of the most serious topics imaginable. This is an essential guide for conversations that really matter."

Reggie Joiner, founder/CEO of Orange, a division of the reThink Group and author of *A New Kind of Leader*

"*Tough Stuff Parenting* is the book every parent needs. With practical tips, deep theological insights, and real-life stories, it will help you feel equipped and ready to engage in some of the most important cultural conversations of our time."

Mandy Arioto, president/CEO of MOPS International

"Paul and Jim bring their considerable wisdom, biblical insight, and life experience to bear on critical issues. If I were a pastor, I'd make sure every parent in my church had a copy of this book…and I'd preach it too! *Tough Stuff Parenting* will strengthen our family bonds and help us leave a legacy of kids and grandkids who follow Jesus and make a kingdom impact in our world."

Reggie McNeal, author of *Kingdom Come*

"If you already have all the answers to the tough questions of parenting, you don't need this book—and I'm sure your kids will turn out awesome! For the rest of us, we now have this amazingly helpful resource. Solid, godly wisdom awaits you inside these pages. You'll breathe easier when the tough stuff comes, and as you apply what you've learned, I'm sure your kids will, indeed, turn out awesome."

Jenny L. Cote, author of *The Amazing Tales of Max and Liz*

"As a father of seven, I found *Tough Stuff* to be a great resource—one I wish I'd had many years ago. Pick up this book, and you'll have the 'teacher's edition' to the unforeseen quizzes parents face every day with their children."

William Vanderbloemen, founder/CEO of Vanderbloemen Search Group

"Practical. Down-to-earth. Extremely relevant. Balanced. As a parent, these are a few of the words I thought of as I read *Tough Stuff Parenting*. The authors don't present an unreachable model of parenting, but rather provide easy-to-grasp principles that can be applied when parenting kids at any age."

Tim Stevens, vice president of consulting for Vanderbloemen Search Group
and author of *Marked by Love*

"Using biblical instruction, Paul Basden and Jim Johnson tackle the really tough stuff of parenting. This is also a good resource for grandparents, as more grandparents are raising grandchildren full-time and need current, up-to-date information on problems their grandkids will likely encounter. I highly recommend this book—as an author, as a parent, and as a grandparent."

Denise George, bestselling author

"Raising kids can be tough, period. It's even tougher in a culture that seems to have lost its moral compass. Jim and Paul, my pastors, provide insightful, practical, biblical wisdom for parents knee-deep in raising their kids to be faithful in these challenging times. If you want to be a step ahead when your kids start asking questions about hot-button issues, you need this book!"

Logan Stout, entrepreneur and founder of IDLife

"Paul Basden and Jim Johnson take on some of the biggest parenting issues and provide relevant responses. In this book, you'll find conversation starters that make talking with your kids easier and a framework for getting beyond the 'what and why' to the 'how and when.' Be ready for some surprising perspectives as you prepare for one of your most important roles as a parent."

Kristen Ivy, author and executive director of messaging for the reThink Group

# Tough Stuff
# PARENTING

## PAUL BASDEN & JIM JOHNSON

HARVEST HOUSE PUBLISHERS
EUGENE, OREGON

Cover design by Bryce Williamson

Published in association with WordServe Literary Group, Ltd., www.wordserveliterary.com.

This book contains stories in which people's names and some details have been changed.

**Tough Stuff Parenting**
Copyright © 2019 by Paul Basden and Jim Johnson
Published by Harvest House Publishers
Eugene, Oregon 97408
www.harvesthousepublishers.com

ISBN 978-0-7369-7506-3 (pbk.)
ISBN 978-0-7369-7507-0 (eBook)

Library of Congress Cataloging-in-Publication Data
Names: Basden, Paul, 1955– author.
Title: Tough stuff parenting / Paul Basden and Jim Johnson.
Description: Eugene, Oregon : Harvest House Publishers, [2018]
Identifiers: LCCN 2018026623 (print) | LCCN 2018029264 (ebook) | ISBN 9780736975070 (ebook) | ISBN 9780736975063 (pbk.)
Subjects: LCSH: Parenting—Religious aspects. | Parent and child.
Classification: LCC BL625.8 (ebook) | LCC BL625.8 .B3 2018 (print) | DDC 248.8/45—dc23
LC record available at https://lccn.loc.gov/2018026623

**Printed in the United States of America**
18 19 20 21 22 23 24 25 26 / VP-GL / 10 9 8 7 6 5 4 3 2 1

### From Paul

*To my wife, Denise:*

*You are the most fun-loving, game-playing,*
*life-celebrating person I know.*

*What a gift to be on the journey with you.*

*And to my daughters, Kari and Kristen:*

*We love you, are proud of you, and have sought to*
*raise you with grace and wisdom.*

*As we've told you all along: "We're doing the best we can.*
*Where we've messed up, we'll pay for counseling."*

### From Jim

*To my parents, James Roy and Vernell Johnson,*
*whose unconditional love marked me forever*

*To my wife, Robin, whose smile captured my heart*
*and has yet to let it go*

*And to my three sons, Benjamin, Tyler, and Brady, whose passion*
*and perseverance for storming castles makes me proud*

# Acknowledgments

We are thankful beyond words to Allison Harrell for her constant help and support of this book. She has served on the Preston Trail staff with us longer than anyone else, she excels in every role she undertakes, and she always has our backs. Allison transcribed several sermons we preached on these topics over the years. She read the manuscript at every stage of development, offering wise suggestions for improvement. She wrote "Breaking It Down for Every Age" at the end of each chapter—a great contribution to the book that flows out of her own firsthand experience of raising four kids. Finally, she has been a constant encourager. Nobody has believed in this book and its potential for blessing families more than Allison. ALH, we treasure you.

We are grateful to John Kramp of HarperCollins, longtime friend from college and seminary days, who read the earliest version of the book and offered endless encouragement when we needed it most.

We thank WordServe Literary for being our agents. Greg Johnson and Keely Boeving have represented us well in the world of publishing, primarily by giving us a chance and by finding us a good publisher. We appreciate their commitment to us and to our first cowriting project.

We are grateful to Harvest House for publishing *Tough Stuff Parenting*. Kyle Hatfield, Gene Skinner, and their talented and gifted team have worked diligently to make this work the best it can be. It is better because of their editing and oversight.

Finally, we want to thank the parents at Preston Trail Community Church for letting us influence you as you've influenced your kids to be world-changing followers of Jesus Christ. You've listened to our messages on these topics, discerned next steps for your families under the Spirit's leadership, and experienced God's favor along the way. We are privileged to be your pastors.

*Jim Johnson and Paul Basden*

# Contents

# Introduction

Jim Johnson

Remember back in high school when the teacher told you to close your books and pull out a pen and a piece of paper? You knew what was coming—the dreaded pop quiz. Your palms started sweating, and your heart began racing as waves of panic swept over you. Moments later, your inner monologue kicked in:

"Why didn't I pay attention in class?"

"You could at least have scanned the chapter, you dummy!"

"I'm doomed...there goes my GPA!"

Looking back, a pop quiz probably didn't keep you out of the college of your choice, but it sure could shoot your anxiety level through the roof. What a relief it was at graduation when that little voice inside said, "Whew, no more pop quizzes."

And then you had children.

How quickly that pop quiz panic returns when your nine-year-old asks, "Mom, you and Dad aren't ever going to get a divorce, are you?" Or your twelve-year-old wonders aloud, "Dad, why does God allow earthquakes to kill so many people?" Or when your sixteen-year-old daughter returns from a sleepover and stuns you by asking, "Mom, when do you think I should go on birth control? Most of my friends are already on it and are having sex with their boyfriends." Or when your son comes home from his first semester at college and reasons, "Dad, if I had been born in Dubai, wouldn't I be a Muslim?"

If you've got young kids, you probably realize these questions are coming very soon. You can already see the wheels turning in their little heads, and you know it's only a matter of time. Plus, you've heard other parents' horror stories, and you want to be proactive. You want to stay at least one step ahead of your kids.

If your kids are older, you may have already been asked questions like these. Your kids took you by surprise, and you weren't ready. Truth be told, you panicked a bit. And your answers...well, they were all over the place. You weren't very convincing to your child or even to yourself. You're determined to be better prepared next time.

We understand. That's why Paul and I wrote this book. We want to help you get ready.

Our work is based on the convergence of two other resources we want to open to you—the Bible and our life experiences. As you read, you will notice that we always turn your attention back to the Bible. It doesn't directly address a lot of the questions children dredge up, but it points us to God and his way of living. Jesus put it like this in what many call his Great Commandment:

> One of them, an expert in religious law, tried to trap him with this question: "Teacher, which is the most important commandment in the law of Moses?"
>
> Jesus replied, "'You must love the LORD your God with all your heart, all your soul, and all your mind.' This is the first and greatest commandment. A second is equally important: 'Love your neighbor as yourself.' The entire law and all the demands of the prophets are based on these two commandments" (Matthew 22:35-40 NLT).

What Jesus reveals to us is this: All the principles, laws, and commands in the Scriptures are examples of what it means to love God fully and love our neighbors as we love ourselves. The Bible couldn't possibly address every question because it was written in a unique historical context. But the Bible clearly points us to the One and the

Way who is timeless and leads us and our children to the abundant and full life Jesus describes.

The second resource I mentioned is the open book of our lives. Paul Basden and I are co-senior pastors of Preston Trail Community Church, located in one of the fastest-growing and most kid-centric cities in the United States: Frisco, Texas. Each month, more than 5,000 parents make their way through the doors of our church, and like you, they are struggling to find some sure handles that will help them guide their children through crucial spiritual and moral issues.

My wife, Robin, and I have raised three sons. Paul and his wife, Denise, have raised two daughters. Our children are all on their own journeys and, with various rates of speed and success, are pursuing the lives to which God is calling them. The good news about our kids is that even though they have taken courses along the way that we would have not chosen, the relationships have remained intact. Today they are not only our children but also beloved friends.

In these chapters, we open up about our lives and share some of our best and worst moments of parenting. As it usually goes, our negative examples will probably be most memorable and helpful, so we offer them in the hope that you can avoid our pitfalls and mistakes. We don't think for a minute that we had all the right answers when we were raising our kids, and we're certain we don't have them all now. But it's our prayer that we can point you in the right direction to get the information you need, help you discover an effective approach to answering the tough questions your children will ask, and ultimately get you on your way to equipping them to lead faithful lives as they grow into young adulthood.

## A Quick Aside About the Book

Paul and I cofounded our church in 2002 and have shared the yoke of leadership and teaching since the beginning. Clearly, this is not the norm, and people often ask us about the arrangement and how it works. After sharing our usual bullet points in response, we close by saying, "Between the two of us, we make one pretty good senior pastor." Paul and I both feel that this has been the most productive and satisfying chapter in our ministry lives. And we think our people have benefited greatly from our partnership in the gospel too—especially by hearing God's truth communicated regularly from our unique perspectives. This is our hope for this book as well.

You will notice that one of us is the primary author of each chapter. Our goal is to identify a high-stakes issue and then bring relevant biblical texts into the discussion. We then offer possible approaches you can use as you interact with your children. We recognize that you will have to apply our guidance in different ways and at different times to fit the age and maturity level of your children. We have provided some helpful tips at the end of each chapter that are broken down by age group and are designed to help you think through how to proceed and get the conversations started. So whether you read the book straight through or dig into the chapters most pertinent to you, we hope this book will help you navigate this crazy world of parenting.

1

# The Bible

## Paul Basden

Richard Lederer is a funny guy. But all his humor is borrowed. Armed with a PhD in English, he has taught the Bible to high school students for almost three decades. After sharing some of the zany test answers he has received, he found out he wasn't alone—teachers from around the country started sending him wacky answers their students had submitted. When he compiled them into one essay, the results were surprising, startling, and ultimately hilarious—especially if the students thought their answers were factual! Several years ago, he published a compilation of his favorite Bible bloopers written by students. Here is a sample.

- In the first book of the Bible, Guinessis, God got tired of creating the world, so he took the Sabbath off. Adam and Eve were created from an apple tree. One of their children, Cain, asked, "Am I my brother's son?"
- Noah's wife was called Joan of Ark.
- Lot's wife was a pillar of salt by day but a ball of fire by night.
- The Jews were a proud people, and throughout history they had trouble with the unsympathetic Genitals.

- Jesus enunciated the Golden Rule, which says to do one to others before they do one to you. He also explained, "Man doth not live by sweat alone."
- The people who followed the Lord were called the 12 decibels. The epistles were the wives of the apostles. One of the opossums was St. Matthew, who was by profession a taximan.
- St. Paul preached holy acrimony, which is another name for marriage. A Christian should have only one wife. This is called monotony.[1]

Perhaps you have never been that biblically illiterate. But if you have ever tried to talk to your kids about biblical matters, you know it can be a tough conversation.

## Why Is It So Hard?

If you're struggling to have great conversations about the Bible with your kids, rest assured you're not alone. But why is it so difficult to discuss the Bible with your children? One answer stands above all others: The Bible is a tough book to understand. Even Simon Peter, who walked and talked with Jesus, said as much.

> Bear in mind that our Lord's patience means salvation, just as our dear brother Paul also wrote you with the wisdom that God gave him. He writes the same way in all his letters, speaking in them of these matters. His letters contain some things that are hard to understand (2 Peter 3:15-16).

If a disciple from Jesus's inner circle confessed that even he struggled to understand the writings of the apostle Paul, we're in good company when we have biblical comprehension problems.

Another reason it's hard to talk to kids about the Bible is that kids can ask tough questions. Here are a dozen doozies asked by children like yours:

- Why did God create the world?
- Who created God?
- Were there dinosaurs on the ark?
- What does God look like?
- Does God have friends, or is he alone?
- Where does God live?
- Does God sleep or rest?
- Does God cry?
- How can Jesus fit into my heart?
- Is there a McDonald's in heaven?
- Why did God make mosquitoes?
- Is Santa Claus God's really rich brother?[2]

I will never forget the Sunday morning I got stumped after worship by a fifth-grader who asked to speak with me. We had no sooner sat down in the atrium than she asked, "If God knows all things, then why did God let Adolf Hitler come to power and eventually kill more than six million Jews?" Her parents had already tried their best to offer an acceptable answer, but she was not satisfied. So they sent her to me. Even with eight years of theological graduate study, I found myself at a loss for words. What does one say, what *can* one say, in the face of such a profound question? I may have given her a few helpful insights, but the age-old dilemma she articulated remained a mystery. She went home that day with her question unanswered.

Realizing these two difficulties, I have two aims in this chapter. The first is to equip you to talk to your kids about the Bible, God, and what Christians have historically believed—regardless of who initiates the discussion. The second is to provide assurance that the Bible can help you find intellectually satisfying and morally clarifying answers to the big questions in your own life, which in turn will prepare your discussions with your kids.

## The Bible Is a Big Book

Of all the things you can tell your children about the Bible, I believe this is the most important: The Bible is God's big book that tells God's big story. That's more than a mouthful, so let's break it down.

Literally, the Bible is a really big book! It doesn't matter if it's the NIV or NLT or KJV translation, paperback or hardback or even online...the Bible is a large, long, and laborious piece of literature. The typical English version has about 800,000 words on 2,000 pages in small print. It's likely bigger and longer than any other book you own or have read.

Here is a high-level summary of what you will read when you open your Bible.

- The first three-fourths is called the Old Testament, or the Jewish Scriptures. It tells about God's creation of the world and his formation of Israel as his chosen nation to bless the world.
- The last one-fourth is called the New Testament, or the Christian Scriptures. It tells about God sending Jesus into the world, followed by God sending the Holy Spirit and the church into the world to continue the work of Jesus.
- The Bible has two testaments (or better, two covenants) but only one God. The God of Abraham, Isaac, and Jacob is none other than the God and Father of our Lord Jesus Christ. When Jesus prayed to his Father in heaven, he was praying to the same God to whom Moses and David and Esther prayed.
- The Bible is composed of 66 books written by more than 40 authors across a span of 1,200 years (from 1100 BC to AD 100). It's more of a library or anthology than a book.

We believe all 66 books of the Bible are inspired by God, but we don't believe all books or passages are equal in usefulness, relevance, or applicability. For example, the New Testament Gospels of

Matthew and Mark are easy to read, they are filled with exciting and inspirational stories and teachings, and they are helpful for following Christ daily. But the same cannot be said for the Old Testament books of Leviticus or Lamentations. Without considerable knowledge of Hebrew history and culture, those books make little sense to today's reader. So I never recommend that someone start reading the Bible wherever they choose and expect that it will be a profitable exercise. If you begin reading randomly, you may end up stopping for good. In the Old Testament especially, it's just too easy to get bogged down in ancestry trees, land assignments, and kosher laws.

The Bible is indeed a big book—in many ways. It can be intimidating if you don't know your way around it. But what makes it worth reading and studying is this: We believe it is God's book.

## The Bible Is God's Book

Prepare to be misunderstood when you say this. Your child will think you're saying that God literally wrote a literal book. Kids think concretely. That's how their minds work. And that won't change until they're well out of childhood. Their brains can't fathom abstract answers until their teen years, and even then, their frontal lobes are just beginning to develop. When a younger child hears that the Bible is God's book, he or she may say, "I get it! God wrote the Bible just like Daddy writes a list, Mommy writes a note, or I write on my tablet. God just used a really big pencil to put the words on the pages."

An older child may conclude, "I'll bet God handwrote the Bible on some kind of non-decomposable paper and then dropped it from heaven to earth. Or maybe God spelled it all out in the skies like a skywriter, and then someone took a picture of it with their smartphone and downloaded it to a Word document. And that's how we got the Bible."

Don't be surprised or shocked at this kind of literal thinking—it's what we should expect from our children. It's normal. It's how God wired their brains. Once you've heard their ideas, you can go on to explain what you mean when you say the Bible is God's book.

First, you mean it's all about God. He's the main character. Hundreds of other human characters are highlighted, including Adam and Eve, Cain and Abel, Abraham and Sarah, Isaac and Jacob, Moses and Aaron, Ruth and Esther, David and Solomon, Elijah and Elisha, Mary and Joseph, Peter and Andrew, James and John, and Paul and Silas. But remind your kids that in every Bible book and Scripture story, the main character is always God. This insight alone will help you talk to your children with clarity.

Second, the Bible is God's book because God inspired it. This is not the same as a country music song being inspired by a bad breakup or a bar brawl. (I'm remembering the classic lyric "I wouldn't take her to a dog fight, not even if she had a chance to win.") Rather, God inspired the Bible in the sense that he guided many writers, over multiple centuries, to write down his mighty deeds of redemption. Without overriding their distinct style of communication, God stimulated and supervised their thoughts and words so that they penned what future generations would need to know about who this God really is. God planned for the personalities of the authors to shine through their writings, but ultimately they wrote what God wanted us to know. In this broad sense, we speak of God being the final author of the Bible and the Scriptures having divine author-ity.

In summary, the Bible is God's big book—it is his gift to us so that we can know him and his purposes. It is not a book of fables or fairy tales, filled with phony stories beginning with "Once upon a time" and ending with "And they all lived happily ever after." It is neither a good-luck charm you carry to ward off evil or misfortune nor a textbook for science, history, economics, or mathematics. It is God's book, God's Word, and God's message to us. It is God's way of revealing himself to humans so we can know who he is in a personal way.

## The Bible Tells Us God's Story

If you're familiar with the Bible, you may object, "The Bible is not one big story. It's a collection of dozens of little stories." In many ways, you would be right. The Bible is filled with hundreds of rich and riveting narratives. In it you will find the stories of creation, humanity's fall into sin, the first murder, the flood, the call of Abraham to father a new nation, the exodus from Egypt, inhabiting the Promised Land, inept judges, countless kings, courageous prophets...and that's just the Old Testament! The New Testament records Jesus's humble birth, eye-popping miracles, and sharp conflicts with religious leaders; his cruel crucifixion and triumphant resurrection from the grave; and the start of the early church, which against all odds, permeated the Greco-Roman world with the good news of God's kingdom made available in Jesus.

But behind all the individual stories is one big story. It is this big story that connects the dots and makes sense of all the small stories. If I had to boil the big story down to one short phrase, it would be this: God is redeeming the world through his Son, Jesus! It is Jesus who gives us the key to understanding the big story in the Bible.

We see this clearly at the end of Luke's Gospel, where the risen Jesus is leading his followers into a profound new understanding of himself.

> He said to them, "This is what I told you while I was still with you: Everything must be fulfilled that is written about me in the Law of Moses, the Prophets and the Psalms." Then he opened their minds so they could understand the Scriptures. He told them, "This is what is written: The Messiah will suffer and rise from the dead on the third day, and repentance for the forgiveness of sins will be preached in his name to all nations, beginning at Jerusalem" (Luke 24:44-47).

Jesus couldn't have been more pointed. The eternal purpose of

God is to redeem the world through his Son. The Old Testament points forward (though not clearly) to Jesus and ultimately finds its fulfillment in him. The New Testament points backward (with great clarity) to Jesus and shows his central role in reconciling the world to God through his sacrificial death and supernatural resurrection.

When you talk to your kids about the Bible, try not to get sidetracked by the details of each individual story and forget the big story. The big story is first and foremost about God, who has revealed himself last and best through Jesus the Messiah.

## Remember Your Crucial Role

Out of his goodness and grace, God has invited us parents to play a major role in the training of the next generation in his ways. That means we must know the Scriptures well if we are going to teach our children well.

Immediately prior to entering the Promised Land, Moses explained to the Israelite parents what God expected of them in training their children to know and follow biblical truth.

> Listen, O Israel! The LORD is our God, the LORD alone. And you must love the LORD your God with all your heart, all your soul, and all your strength. And you must commit yourselves wholeheartedly to these commands that I am giving you today. Repeat them again and again to your children. Talk about them when you are at home and when you are on the road, when you are going to bed and when you are getting up again (Deuteronomy 6:4-7 NLT).

These words still apply to parents today, as do the words of Paul the apostle when he provided parenting instructions to believers in the early church: "Fathers, do not exasperate your children; instead, bring them up in the training and instruction of the Lord" (Ephesians 6:4).

God entrusts to parents the primary responsibility of raising their children—to teach them to love the Lord and follow his ways. As you consider this sacred opportunity, let me offer encouragement, warning, and hope.

First the encouragement: If you will do your part, God will do his part...and more! Your part is to faithfully teach and model for your children what it means to be a Christ-follower in today's world. God's part is to empower and animate your words and actions so that your children see Christ in you, are drawn to Christ in you, and want to follow Christ for themselves. God will always do his part when you do your part.

Next the warning: You have just one chance to raise your kids. The average parent has 18 years to make an eternal impact on their children before the kids leave home and strike out on their own. You have only one life, and your child has only one life. How you use your life to raise your child is crucial. You can't raise your kids without a spiritual rudder and then suddenly call for a do-over if they morally capsize at age 18. None of us can wipe the slate clean and start over again.

But there is hope. No one is perfect, especially when it comes to parenting. We can't turn the clock back—but God can always redeem our mess-ups. Second chances and new beginnings are what grace is all about. When my daughters were teenagers, they tried my patience more than once. At times I lost my cool or said or even yelled words I regretted. And yes, I told both of them I would pay for their counseling when they got older and needed therapy for any daddy-daughter wounds I had inflicted. The hope of parenting is not that we will do it all right, but that God will somehow make it all right by the power of grace.

If you want to impact your kids for Jesus, both in this life and for eternity, then take seriously God's invitation to teach your children well. Make it a priority. Let it become as important to you as eating three meals a day, using deodorant each morning, or checking your

Facebook news feed regularly. It must become a fixed, consistent, valuable part of your daily life.

Knowing how crucial your role as a parent truly is, here are some steps to take on the road to family discipleship.

## Read the Bible for Yourself

We've all heard, "You can't take someone where you haven't been." In the context of raising your children, here's what it means: If you want to help your children explore the wonderful world of the Bible, you must know it yourself. You must read the Bible on your own.

How do you start? Here are some specific ideas I have practiced over the years that have made a remarkable difference for me. They aren't original, but they have helped me better understand the Bible and, in turn, know and love the God revealed in the Bible.

### Choose a modern translation.

English translations have never been more accessible or user-friendly than they are today. I prefer reading the New International Version (NIV) or New Living Translation (NLT). Some of my more artistic and creative friends like to read the poetic paraphrase of the Bible by Eugene Peterson called The Message. Don't get hung up on translations—just find one and read it.

### Select a format you enjoy.

You may favor the traditional hard copy Bible with a cover on the outside and pages on the inside because for you there's something sacred about holding the Scriptures in your hands. Conversely, you may prefer to read the Bible from an electronic device with internet access, such as your smartphone or tablet. God doesn't have a preference of format. He just wants you to be still, be quiet, and prayerfully read from the layout that helps you most.

### Follow a daily Bible reading plan.

If you want to design your own plan, I recommend starting with the Psalms and Proverbs in the Old Testament and the four Gospels,

Acts, and James in the New Testament. Those eight books will almost always connect you to God. Begin with any one of them, and you will see what I mean. If you prefer a predesigned reading plan, you can utilize online tools or apps, such as Bible Study Tools, Bible Gateway, or YouVersion. They feature several approaches to help you enjoy reading a portion of the Bible each day.

### Find a regular time and place to read your Bible.

Your life stage will influence what time and place works best for you right now, but beware of making too many excuses—they may indicate you are trying to avoid meeting with God. My wife and I have two adult daughters, so we have the freedom of reading the Bible every morning in our den without fear of being interrupted by the pitter-patter of little feet. We sit in separate chairs; she has her Bible reading plan, and I have mine. We commonly interrupt each other to share what God is teaching us. I love meeting my wife and the Lord each morning with a cup of coffee in one hand and my Bible in the other. It's among my favorite moments of every day.

Of course, if your kids are younger, you will have to be creative in finding time to read God's Word. You may be able to find a few moments here and there in the nooks and crannies of the day—those small segments of five or ten minutes when there is minimal chaos and a whisper of peace. Grab those moments as gifts from God and read a few verses for inspiration and strength!

### Read slowly and thoughtfully.

This advice may seem counterintuitive at first, but it's crucial. In our fast-paced world, we often scan rapidly rather than read carefully. For some things, rapid reading is fine. But when it comes to the Bible, less is more. It takes time to get used to the rhythm and flow of Scripture—it's unlike anything else you read. I always say God doesn't give extra credit for speed-reading. In fact, just the opposite—he reveals himself to those who linger unhurriedly and pause to ponder the Word before them. When you invest in thoughtfully reading the Word of God, your return will be a personal experience of the presence of God.

### Read with your spiritual eyes open.

The human spirit is where we connect with God's Spirit.[3] It is where, as my father used to say, we "do business with God." Having a receptive spirit means you freely ask God to reveal to you any sins you need to avoid, any promises you need to claim, any examples you need to follow, and any commands you need to obey. As you open yourself to God's book before you, you are fully committed to being an open book before God. Such openness is modeled in the prayer that concludes Psalm 139: "Search me, God, and know my heart; test me and know my anxious thoughts. See if there is any offensive way in me, and lead me in the way everlasting" (Psalm 139:23-24).

### Memorize and meditate on passages that speak to you.

I began memorizing Bible verses in college when our campus minister challenged me to learn two verses a week for the whole semester. I did it successfully, so I tried it again the next semester. And then the next. By the time I graduated, I had well over 100 Bible verses committed to memory. Sadly, I can't seem to memorize Bible verses as easily today as I could back then, but the ones I memorized back then are still with me today. They help me think like God thinks. They help me appropriate Jesus's "mental map" into my way of thinking.[4] You have to know what Jesus is thinking if you want to follow him.

Those seven ideas can help you read the Bible for yourself and become a lover of God's Word. Then you will be excited about taking your children where you've been.

## Read the Bible to or with Your Kids

If your children are too young to read, you can read the Bible to them aloud. If they're old enough to read, you can read it with them.

Either way, I recommend using a children's version of the Bible. Our grandsons are learning from *The Jesus Storybook Bible*.[5] We also love *The Bible App for Kids*, an interactive online children's Bible produced by YouVersion.[6]

As to the best time to read the Bible to or with your children, many parents have discovered that bedtime is the best time. It's when many kids are most receptive and open to your influence. When our daughters were young, we tried reading the Bible to them at breakfast, but between them being sleepyheads and us feeling the pressure to get them out the door and to school on time, it was a challenge. So we changed our plan. We moved Bible reading to bedtime, and that is when we had the most success. That is when they were quiet, lying down, and open to spiritual things.

## Talk to Them About the Bible

This is more than just reading the Bible to or with them. This includes asking them to share what they heard or learned during the reading time. You may be surprised at what they say—children can listen while they're fiddling with their bedcovers or spinning like a top. So listen carefully, because their words provide a peek into the window of their souls. Kids have not yet learned to be people pleasers or image polishers, so they say what's on their minds. Their words will tell you where God is working in their lives. But you must ask them.

Some parents fear this means they have to be Bible-answer experts. Not true. You simply have to be on the journey yourself. Share what you can, and don't be afraid to say, "I don't know, but let's try to find the answer together." Blessed are the parents who have heart-to-heart conversations with their children about spiritual matters.

## Pray the Bible with Them

"Praying the Bible" may sound like a strange phrase, but it simply means praying with your kids about what you just read. So when you read with them about courage or faith or honesty or God's peace, let those topics inform the prayers you say with your kids. You will be leading your children in a two-way conversation with their heavenly Father—first they listen to him speak through Scripture, and then they speak to him though prayer. As Mark Batterson says, "The Bible is not meant to be read through—it's meant to be prayed through."[7]

## Conclusion

When your kids want to know about the Bible, tell them it's God's big book that tells God's big story. But don't stop there! Commit yourself to reading and loving God's Word so you can become the kind of Christ-follower who naturally reads and talks about and prays the Bible with your kids. As I look back on my childhood, I realize that my parents read the Bible to me daily when I was growing up. After I got married, my wife and I did the same with our daughters. Now our oldest daughter has three boys and reads God's Word to them every day. I am thankful for the promise found in Exodus 20:6, which I have seen come true in my life and family for three consecutive generations: "I lavish unfailing love for a thousand generations on those who love me and obey my commands" (NLT).

*Dear Lord,*

*You've entrusted us with one of the biggest jobs in the world—raising our kids so they will find and follow Jesus Christ. As parents, we know our task is to lead them to love your Word so they can know and love you forever. But we also feel the heaviness of this role. On our own, we are totally inept. But in your strength, we trust that we will be competent to read, discuss, and pray the Scriptures with our children. Help us then, Father, to love our kids the way you love them, to point them to Jesus as Savior and Lord, and to grow in our own faith so we can help them grow in theirs.*

*Amen.*

## Breaking It Down for Every Age

The Bible isn't just another big book lining the family bookshelf—it's God's big book. The best way to answer the question "What do I tell my kids about the Bible?" is to read it for ourselves and grow in our own knowledge of and love for the God revealed in its pages.

### Elementary-Aged Kids

Don't miss the opportunity during these young years to help your kids develop a foundational understanding of the Bible as God's big book. Identify the best time of day to read the Bible with your child. Choose a version that will capture his or her attention and imagination, such as *The Jesus Storybook Bible* or *The Complete Illustrated Children's Bible*, and make that habit a part of your regular family rhythm. If your family attends church, your child will learn about heroes from the Bible, such as Abraham, Moses, David, and Paul. Help them understand that all these important people are supporting characters in God's big book. Sometimes they made wise choices, and sometimes they made foolish choices, but the significance of their stories is found in their connection to God, the Bible's main character. All their stories matter because of the role they play in the overarching narrative of how much God loves us and wants a relationship with us. Help your kids come to know that God is the main character of the Bible and that he has revealed himself most clearly through his Son, Jesus.

### Tweens

During the tween years, life becomes more complicated. Suddenly schoolwork is more challenging, friendships are more treacherous, and peer pressure is more intense. One of the greatest gifts you can offer your tween during this stressful season is to help him connect real life with God's Word. When he comes to you with an issue or concern, listen. Empathize. But don't miss the opportunity to point your tween back to the Bible. Help him identify a key verse that speaks comfort, encouragement, or wisdom into the situation. Take the time to pray that verse with your preteen and encourage him to memorize it as well. Committing Bible verses to memory during this season of life will help establish a firm foundation in God's Word that will yield blessings far into the future.

## Teens

During the teen years, your child will be preparing to launch from your home and into a culture that generally regards the Bible as irrelevant to real life. Help your teen place her confidence in the Bible by encouraging her to build a relationship with Jesus. Countless age-appropriate resources are available for Bible study—find one that piques your teen's interest and points her toward the Gospels. You may feel as if your child prefers to keep you at arm's length during these years, but she is likely hungry for your undivided attention. If she is open to it, offer to study the Bible with your teen and prioritize a weekly time and place for that to happen—maybe a local coffee shop or other favorite hangout. Helping her grow to love the Bible doesn't mean having all the answers but instead having a willingness to learn and grow alongside her. If your teen would respond better to a Bible study with peers in a small group setting, help her connect with small group resources offered by your local church.

## Questions for Personal Reflection or Group Discussion

1. How much of God's big story have you explained to your child?
2. What would need to change in your schedule for you to be able to read the Bible to or with your child every evening?
3. Have you tried any Bible reading plans to connect with God? If so, were they helpful? If not, what plan sounds good to you that you could start soon?

4. Do you have a regular time and place to meet God daily and read his Word? If not, when and where would you like to start?

## Additional Resources

If you are interested in further reading on this subject, these resources may be helpful.

### For Parents

*The Reason for God* by Tim Keller (chapter 7)

*Understanding the Bible* (expanded edition) by John R.W. Stott

*The Bible Jesus Read* by Philip Yancey

### For Children and Teens

*The Complete Illustrated Children's Bible* by Janice Emmerson-Hicks

*The Jesus Storybook Bible* by Sally Lloyd-Jones

*The Student Bible*

*The Student Bible Dictionary* (expanded and updated edition) by Johnnie Godwin and Phyllis Godwin

# 2

# Partying

## Jim Johnson

It started out as one of the finest weekends of our 20-year parenting career. On Thursday evening, the youngest of our three sons was crowned "Mr. Spartan" at his eighth-grade award ceremony. The award recipient was selected by students and teachers, recognizing the outstanding leader and student in their class. As he stepped up to receive his reward, my wife, Robin, and I were quietly and humbly patting ourselves on the back for parenting such a budding prodigy.

Little did we know that within 36 hours we would no longer be parenting a prodigy, but a prisoner. It started with a seemingly innocuous invitation to a friend's fourteenth birthday party. Brady told us he was invited to the overnight birthday party and asked if he could go. I reminded him that he had an important basketball game the next day at noon and that he owed his teammates his best effort. We agreed that around midnight he would find a quiet place and go to sleep so he would be well rested for the next day. He assured me I could trust him.

At 1:45 a.m. I was shocked into consciousness by the phone ringing next to my pillow. On the other end of the line I heard Brady's sheepish, hesitant voice. "Dad, I'm so sorry. I let you down. I need you to come and pick me up at the party…and the police will be here when you arrive."

You can imagine the thoughts racing through my mind as I hurriedly made the 40-minute drive to one of the most exclusive and security-minded gated neighborhoods in the northern suburbs of Atlanta. When I pulled up to the party's host home, I was stunned to find five Gwinnett County police cars and the canine unit parked in front. (I would later learn that the police helicopter had already returned to its pad.)

As it turned out, 21 boys, all 14 years old, were at the overnight party. Only two adults were there to supervise. That things got out of control is not surprising. Around nine that night, Brady and a couple of friends slipped away from the party and went ding-dong ditching (ringing doorbells and running) in the neighborhood. Not terribly smart but not unusual for young teens. They made their critical error, however, when for some reason they decided to go back to the same residence multiple times. On the final ring, a middle-aged man and his adult son bolted out of the house with a PVC pipe in hand, caught one of Brady's friends, and started beating him with the pipe. (PVC is plastic, so no major damage was done.)

Brady and his other friend ran into the piney woods and made their escape. They spent the next two hours on the lam in the woods and ravines of the subdivision as the Gwinnett County Police Department—which had been called by the PVC guy—amassed just about every asset at their disposal (except the SWAT team!) to track them down. Thinking they were in the clear, Brady and his accomplice slipped in the back way to their friend's home, where much to their surprise, a small welcoming party of Gwinnett County police awaited them. With little fanfare, they were arrested for criminal trespassing, and parents were called. So much for the Father of the Year Award I'd imagined just the day before!

Looking back now, the story is funnier than it is tragic, and it probably goes down as the most expensive police operation in history for ding-dong ditching! But it opened my eyes to the knee-buckling challenge of parenting kids through the "party years."

What is it about this phase of parenting that raises our fear and anxiety levels at least another notch? Here's the answer: The party years reveal three of the most crucial challenges parents will face in the teen years.

- How much control are we going to try to exercise over our children and for how long?
- What peer group will our children connect with for their final formative years?
- How is the game of trust going to play out with our kids as we give them more and more freedom before they leave home?

As most of us are aware, a lot is at stake in how successfully we manage these challenges. Our responses will determine to a large degree our kids' emotional health and our relationship with them when they finally launch.

These challenges are complicated by the fact that they don't exist in a vacuum. Some parents bring their own checkered history into these trying years. They live with a lingering regret born of the poor decisions they made in their teen or young adult years. Thus the thought of their kids going down the same path can be paralyzing.

For others, fear spikes because of the unknown. Parents who grew up in conservative homes may have been sheltered from party life. We tend to fear most what we know least, so when we hear horror stories of what goes on at parties, we can quickly pen a story line that projects the absolute worst. Rumors and news stories about rampant chemical abuse, sex games, and casual hookups are enough to traumatize even the best of us!

Biology also appears to be working against us. Neuroscientists now tell us that a child's prefrontal cortex does not fully develop until the late teens or even early twenties. The upshot of this neurological tidbit is that adolescents and even young adults struggle with controlling their emotional responses and identifying the implications of their decisions. Simply put, teens typically make emotionally driven decisions with little or no appreciation for the future negative consequences. A well-known comic was ahead of his time when he declared, "Kids are brain damaged!"

With this being the case, it should come as no surprise that parents often respond in one of two extreme ways. The first, a knee-jerk reaction, is to clamp down hard and declare all parties off-limits, hoping to protect their kids from the partying life as long as they can.

The second approach is what I call a preemptive surrender. The prospect of monitoring and controlling kids' behaviors in today's anything-goes culture seems so overwhelming, it's just easier for parents to convince themselves that the battle is ultimately a lost cause. They raise the white flag, set no boundaries, acquiesce to all invitations, and simply hope and maybe pray for the best.

The good news is that there is a third option. It's neither a rash response nor an outright resignation. It offers genuine hope that we can help our kids make wise decisions about the parties to which they are invited. If we do a good job of walking our kids through this process, the decision-making skills we will help them develop will serve them even after their teen and young adult years are a distant memory. This option includes three steps:

- Bless what is good about a party.
- Be clear about how and when a good party goes bad.
- Help them identify wise choices by asking them thoughtful questions.

The wisdom of this approach becomes apparent as we consider the tension between protecting our children and preparing them to take on more responsibility. When parenting a preschooler, a parent's role is weighted more heavily toward protection than preparation. When children move into elementary school, the situation calls for a more balanced approach. The art of parenting in the teen years is discerning how to adjust these dials and emphasize preparation rather than protection.

## Bless What Is Good About a Party

A good place to start is to assure your kids that God loves a good party! Surprised? Check out the life of Jesus. He went to parties during his time on earth—even the kind of parties you would not want your kids to attend. Prostitutes and other ne'er-do-wells were there. In fact, Jesus gained the reputation of being a glutton and a drunkard because he chose to keep company with these kinds of partiers (see Luke 7:34). Also, he famously rescued the mother of a bride from a shameful wedding faux pas by turning water into wine when the steward recognized the stock was running low. As John records it, he didn't skimp either. He turned six 20- to 30-gallon water pots (enough to fill more than 908 bottles!) into the very finest vintage.[1]

Before the appearance of Jesus, God's affinity for celebrating and partying is clear in the Old Testament descriptions of Israel's feasts and holy days. Deuteronomy 14 contains a little-known (and rarely preached on) passage of Scripture in which God tells the nation of Israel what to do if they live too far away to bring their tithe to one of the sanctioned places.

> Exchange your tithe for silver, and take the silver with you and go to the place the LORD your God will choose. Use the silver to buy whatever you like: cattle, sheep, wine or other fermented drink, or anything you wish. Then you and your household shall eat there in the presence of the LORD your God and rejoice (Deuteronomy 14:25-26).

Surely Moses is misunderstanding his divine promptings. Can God really be saying that if you can't make it to the service, you can use your tithe to throw a family bash? Apparently so. No way around it—God loves watching his children have a good time in his name!

In the book of Revelation, the big story of God's redeeming work in history culminates with a huge wedding feast, where there will be much celebration around a table full of God's richest bounty (Revelation 19:6-9). There you have it. From beginning to end, the Bible tells us God has given us good things to enjoy—good friends, food, music, dancing, and drink—and he does this because he wants us to celebrate his goodness.

The cautious parent in us may grant that God loves a good party, but we wonder, what makes a party good? Simply put, a party is good when we honor God by enjoying his gracious gifts in his name and in his way. When we, as parents, give a gift to our children, we love to see them derive enjoyment from it. In the same way, God loves to see his children enjoying the good gifts he's given. So when we gather with friends on special occasions (or no occasion at all) to share a delicious meal, engaging conversations, music, a dance or two—and we do it with an awareness that everything we are enjoying is a gift from God—then we are partying in a good way, a life-giving way…dare I say, a holy way.

As the writer of Ecclesiastes says, "So I commend the enjoyment of life, because there is nothing better for a person under the sun than to eat and drink and be glad. Then joy will accompany them in their toil all the days of the life God has given them under the sun" (Ecclesiastes 8:15). Sounds like we don't have to have a birthday, a special event, or holiday to kick back with friends and enjoy a good time. An unauthorized Parrot Head paraphrase of this text might be "It's five o'clock somewhere!"

I remember vividly when this truth finally dawned on me. I grew up in a conservative family and church where celebrations were tempered, lest in our joy and abandon we might fall into sin. According to an unspoken rule, the only fare served at a celebration was red fruit punch and cookies. At a really important function, a peanut or mint tray might also be offered. No wonder my capacity to genuinely feel and participate in the enjoyment of God's best gifts was underdeveloped...until Meggie's wedding.

Meggie is the daughter of some of our best friends in Atlanta, Georgia. After I officiated her wedding at the Baptist church, we all made our way to the local country club. This should have been my first clue that the event would feature more than fruit punch and cookies! When we walked into the ballroom, a band was playing, lights were flashing, beef tenderloin dressed the buffet, wine flowed, and champagne corks popped. We watched the new couple dance to their special song, and then their parents cut in to join the fun. When the oohs and ahhs subsided, the bride and her bridesmaids cleared the floor and then stunned the groom and crowd with a choreographed, lip-synced rendition of Britney Spears's "Oops!...I Did It Again." Then for the next three hours, the wedding party, family, and friends ate, drank, danced, laughed, reminisced, took pictures, and offered toasts and blessings. As we did so, there was for me a palpable sense of God's presence. In my heart, God was saying again, "This is good...this is very good!"

When it comes to these good gifts, though, we must issue one caveat. Certainly there are those for whom alcohol, certain foods, or even certain activities are off-limits due to past life issues. The choice to abstain from certain gifts, especially in conjunction with a recovery program, shows wise discernment. And of course, for those who are underage, drinking is not a proper way to celebrate God's gifts. But for responsible adults, the Bible is clear: "To the pure, all things are pure, but to those who are corrupted and do not believe, nothing is pure. In fact, both their minds and consciences are corrupted" (Titus 1:15). The apostle Paul is saying here that whenever we enjoy God's good gifts in his name and following his ways, our purity is not compromised.

One final note. Parents, we encourage you to model a healthy party lifestyle for your kids. Modeling a healthy, biblical way to party may be one of the most effective teaching tools at your disposal.

One couple in the church we co-pastor, Warren and Sonya, have a unique gift of hospitality, and Paul and I love going to their home with our wives and other friends. We can always count on candles, music, and the smell of delicious food. As we sit with our friends and eat, drink, laugh, and share what God is doing in our lives, we are acutely aware of God's goodness and his presence among us.

I once asked Warren about the way he and Sonya model partying around their kids, and he told me they are intentional about bringing their children into the planning of their get-togethers. Together, they discuss the menu and the activities. Sometimes they choose to serve adult beverages and sometimes they don't, because they want their kids to know that a fun party doesn't depend on alcohol. By including their kids in these discussions, Warren and Sonya are not only teaching them hospitality but also demystifying the concept of partying for them. You might say they are teaching their kids how to party well!

## Be Clear About How and When a Party Goes Bad

After you have blessed what's good about a party, you can begin to help your kids recognize when a party goes bad. When it comes to telling the difference between a good party and a bad party, I'm reminded of an old Southern joke.

> Question: How do you tell the difference between "naked" and "nekkid"?
>
> Answer: "Naked" means you don't have any clothes on. "Nekkid" means you don't have any clothes on and you're up to something.

In the same way, there's a party, and then there's a "partay." A party is when you're having some friends over to have a good time. A "partay" is when you're having some friends over to have a good time and you're up to something. More specifically, a "partay" happens when people are enjoying God's good gifts in a way that dishonors him and other partygoers.

When we're left to our own devices, it's easy for a good party to go bad, because we can easily begin to objectify the gifts and disregard both the Giver and the principles he put in place for those gifts. For example, some people might objectify alcohol and go to a party simply to become drunk. The Bible is very clear that drunkenness is sin. The Bible is also very clear that the law of the land is to be our guide, so when minors break the law by drinking alcohol, they sin.

It's possible to go to a party and objectify a person of the opposite sex with the goal of "hooking up." The Bible is very clear that sexual intimacy outside the bounds of a marriage covenant is a sin. Tell your kids that when any of these kinds of things are taking place, look out—a good party has gone bad.

To gain a little more insight as to how good parties go bad in our community, we asked the students in our church to enlighten us. They are good kids, but their responses paint a heartbreaking picture for pastors and parents. Here are just a few.

- "There is almost always alcohol, and it's a lot easier to get drugs than parents realize" (age 16).
- "My friends have accepted a drink they may or may not know was spiked, and the next thing they knew they were in bed with someone they just met" (age 17).
- "Parents would be freaked out about all of the use of marijuana and drinking and also sometimes sex" (age 15).
- "[I see] drinking, smoking (weed, cigarettes, hookah), strip poker, sometimes sexual things" (age 17).
- "Some parties have a Xanax bar—like an alcohol bar but with pills" (age 16).
- "Many parents allow their kids to party as long as they are

honest with them. I know one mom who knows where her kid's bong is and doesn't say anything about it" (age 16).

- "The word 'party' as kids know it these days means to 'get faded' rather than just have a good time" (age 16).
- "Normally it's the kids who have been raised well who do it. You'd never think they would do it" (age 16).

When we read these kinds of things, our "concern meter" hits the red zone. So how should we talk to our kids? How do we prepare them? This question points to the third important thing to tell your kids about partying: Tell them you want to help them make wise choices about partying. Keep in mind that when you hand them the car keys or they leave for college, they're going to make their decisions free from your watchful eye. How well they respond in those situations will be determined largely by how well you have helped them learn to make wise choices.

## Help Your Kids Make Wise Choices

As you think about helping your kids make wise choices about partying, take a moment to reflect on Psalm 90:12: "Teach us to number our days, that we may gain a heart of wisdom." The psalmist is asking God to help him understand his life from a larger perspective. One of our primary callings as parents is to teach our kids how to do this—to understand life from a larger perspective, to number their days. Kids often make decisions with little thought of any negative consequences. As parents, our job is to help them recognize cause-and-effect relationships so they can develop a heart of wisdom.

We can do this by asking them some "wise choice" questions about partying. Before we get to the questions, though, there are two important points to understand. First, these aren't one-off questions. Rather, they are most effective when used as part of your ongoing conversations with your kids. Teens are being tugged by three powerful forces: the pressure of their peers, their inner curiosity and hormonally inspired desires, and their inherent awareness of right and wrong, which God has planted in their hearts. The thought that you can have a one-and-done conversation about what goes on at parties and how your teens should respond is wishful thinking at best. In fact, if this isn't an ongoing conversation in your house well before they're heading out the door to a party, chances are good that these questions won't be received all that well.

Second, when your child chooses unwisely (as he likely will at some point), resist the temptation to jump into your rescue helicopter to swoop in and save the day. Teens' moral sense of judgment will develop only if you allow them to feel the full weight of their actions. When you rescue your child from experiencing the consequences of his own actions, you sabotage this process, and you're only hurting him in the long run.

## "Wise Choice" Questions About a Party

*"Why is it important to you that you go?"*

This may seem like an obvious question, but it's important to understand that kids primarily go to parties for two reasons: They crave acceptance and want to belong, and they want to have fun. How they answer this question may give you a small window into their developing young souls. You may glean some real insight that will guide future conversations you'll want to have.

Don't be surprised, though, if your kids have trouble articulating their whys. They may not yet be able to get in touch with many of the feelings that are ricocheting around in their minds. Plus, being evasive is standard operating procedure for most teenagers. If you can't get them to level with you about why it's so important for them to go to a party, don't despair. Simply asking them the question plants a potent seed in their thought processes. It will germinate sometime in the future, and when it does, they will begin thinking about the reasons and weighing their motivations in their own minds and hearts. And when they do, count it as a really big win!

### "Are you going to influence others or be influenced by them at the party?"

Keeping this value as a topic of conversation may be one of the most important things you can do to prepare your child for her future. Creating a vision in her mind and heart that she is the one God is calling to influence others will serve her well throughout her life!

When I had to pick up Brady from the birthday party gone bad, we obviously needed to have this conversation again. He clearly made the poor decisions that led to that fateful, middle-of-the-night phone call, but we agreed that one of the reasons he was in that predicament was that a classmate had influenced him. This friend knew how to push Brady's buttons, and he consistently brought out the worst in him. After this experience, we did something we had never felt it necessary to do before: We laid down the law that he must break off his relationship with this friend—and he did. As a result, his life changed for the better.

Help your kids identify the friends who call out the best in them and the ones who call out the worst. Be watchful and make your own observations as a parent. Then armed with all that information, decide whether your child can go to the party based on who is going to be there.

### "Will parents be supervising the party?"

This is a vitally important question to ask. If your child assures you that parents will be present, call the parents in advance, especially if you have never met them. Verify they will be there. Ask some questions about their presence at the party. Will they be sealed off upstairs, or will they be actively monitoring the party? How many kids will be there? Will alcohol be allowed—even if the kids are underage? What time will the party be over? It is your prerogative to ask these kinds of questions in advance, and the answers you get will help you talk to your kids about the party.

If after asking these three questions you feel comfortable in allowing him to attend, let me suggest one additional safeguard. Come up with an agreed-upon exit plan with your child in case the party goes bad. Often teens will find themselves in an uncomfortable party situation where they know things aren't right, but they don't know what to do. Think of a way he can leave the situation without losing face in the eyes of his friends.

For example, you might create a "mean parent" plan. Your child texts you with a prearranged message, and you call her back and tell her you're coming to get her. Your child can use you as the excuse to leave. "My parents are so mean. They're going to come get me." Hopefully as she grows older, she will learn to exit bad situations without your assistance, but especially when she is younger and more easily influenced, being perceived as a mean parent by your child's peers is a very small price for you to pay for your child's security.

## Tying It All Together

As you ask these "wise choice" questions, it's also important to talk about appropriate expectations and consequences. This is how our children develop a moral compass. For example, regarding your expectations about the use of alcohol or drugs, it's pretty simple. Our government has created laws regarding the illegal use of controlled substances and a minimum drinking age, and there are potentially severe legal consequences if those laws are broken. At the very minimum, our parental expectations should align with the law of the land.

But many parents have discovered that simply relying on legal statutes is not enough. The law of the land isn't always a sufficiently strong deterrent for underage drinking or illegal drug use. That is why ongoing conversations with your children about these issues even before they enter middle school is so important. During these pre-crisis conversations, you can rationally lay out the reasons they should avoid these behaviors, set your expectations for their behavior, and outline the consequences should they fail to meet them.

Other challenges they will face will not call legal principles into play as much as spiritual ones. Our kids are growing up in a "hookup" culture that pervades even the middle school years. Conversations about sex and appropriate sexual involvement need to happen early and often. If you err, err in telling them too early. Bottom line, you always want your voice to be the first voice your children hear about issues of personal morality.

If you give your child a phone with internet access or they have friends with internet access, it is highly likely they are going to not only hear about sex but also see graphic sexual images on porn sites or from sexts sent by classmates or friends…way before you are ready. The longer you wait to start these conversations and set appropriate boundaries, the greater the risk of dangerous behavior when they start attending parties away from your watchful eye. (For more on this topic, see chapter 4, "Having Sex"; chapter 8, "Porn"; and chapter 10, "Drugs and Alcohol.")

## A Bottom Line for Parents

Instructing our kids, asking them strategic questions, and setting healthy expectations are all important ways to help them make the best decisions about partying. But the bottom line is this: Our personal moral choices are going to speak much louder than any words. So in conjunction with all these conversations, we must decide for ourselves how we're going to approach life's dangerous pleasures.

The reality is that God gives us many dangerous pleasures in life. We can eat too much good food and become a glutton. We can drink too much wine and become an alcoholic. We can take prescription medication after surgery and become an addict. We can earn a good paycheck and become a materialist. Almost any good thing has the potential to go bad when we become obsessed with it. The way we approach these pleasures not only determines the course of our lives but also sets an example for our children.

It is not an easy task to navigate our own way through the moral morass in today's world, much less guide our children. In all things, we would do well to remember that what matters most to Jesus is our hearts.

> Don't you see that whatever enters the mouth goes into the stomach and then out of the body? But the things that come out of a person's mouth come from the heart, and these defile them. For out of the heart come evil thoughts— murder, adultery, sexual immorality, theft, false testimony, slander (Matthew 15:17-19).

As parents, we tend to focus most on what our kids are putting into or wearing on their bodies, and we focus less on the condition of their hearts. But unless their hearts are full of confidence in the love of Christ and your love as their parent, they're going to go out into the world looking for something else to fill that emptiness. The most important thing you can do as a parent is to focus on your children's hearts, continually pointing them to the love and life that only Christ can bring. Proverbs 4:23 captures it best: "Above all else, guard your heart, for everything you do flows from it."

If you want to prepare your kids to manage the party scene well, start with their hearts. If you have not already started talking with them patiently and thoughtfully about their relationships with Christ, begin now. Like no one else, we can help guard our children's hearts by modeling a vital faith, a secure love, and a certain hope.

..........................................................................................

*Dear Lord,*

*Thank you for every good and perfect gift that comes from you. May we receive these good gifts with joy and thanksgiving. Teach us to celebrate you and all you give us, in ways that honor you and increase your reputation in the world. As we invite our children into the joyous celebrations of life, give us wisdom to train them well so they can revel in your goodness and never abandon the Giver for the gift.*

*Amen.*

## Breaking It Down for Every Age

As your kids grow and mature, the meaning of the word "party" begins to change dramatically. What once denoted a sweet family affair with cake and candles may, a few years later, provoke parental concern about the dangers of controlled substances and sexual experimentation. Here are some things to keep in mind as you initiate ongoing conversations with your kids about partying.

### Elementary-Aged Kids

The parties your kids attend during this phase are likely innocuous gatherings, but don't miss the opportunity to initiate conversations that prepare them for their tween and teen years. If alcohol is present in your family's life, help your kids understand its proper place in adult celebrations (and remember, your actions will speak louder than your words). If alcohol is not present in your family's life, help your kids understand why you've made that choice without demonizing alcohol or those who choose to partake.

### Tweens

It is often in the tween phase that kids are first exposed to the kind of party that provokes parental concern. As your child spends more time with his friends away from your home, be sure to employ the "wise choice" questions shared in this chapter. Establish an escape plan with your kid so that, should a good party turn bad, he can call you without fear of punishment.

Your tween's friends are becoming increasingly important in her life, so ask questions about them and then listen to what your child says. Ask about the choices her friends make in their everyday lives, the words she uses with other kids and adults, and whether her friends' behavior is markedly different or the same around different kinds of people. As your tween opens up, keep in mind that your response will determine how much she continues to share with you. Be sure to praise the positive more than you focus on the negative. Notice and affirm the times your kid shows positive leadership among her friends, and talk about what that might look like in every environment—at school, in sports, or just hanging out.

## Teens

Having a teenager means it's time to tweak the dials on your parenting. As you ease up on *protection*, you'll increase *preparation* for the next big phase in his life—adulthood. At times, this can be a frustrating tension to manage, and you may be tempted to respond to the challenge by simply choosing one extreme or the other: overprotect at all costs or throw in the towel and grant adult freedoms too soon. This is likely to be a challenging season, but remember that your teen wants to communicate with you. Engage him in conversations about the difference between a party and a "partay."

And don't underestimate the importance of laughing with your teen. Help her develop an awareness that God is the Creator and Giver of every good gift. He delights in our enjoyment of his gifts, just as he delights in our enjoyment of him. Remind your teen that our role is to enjoy those gifts in ways that bring God delight and praise.

## Questions for Personal Reflection or Group Discussion

1. As you think about your teenage children heading off to a party, what scares you most?

2. As you examine these fears, what experiences from your past are shaping your perceptions and feelings in the present?

3. What kind of parties or celebrations does your family enjoy? What role does God play in those celebrations? Is he invited? Is his presence acknowledged as you celebrate?

4. What boundaries do you want to help your kids set when it comes to parties? How and when should you begin having conversations about them?

5. What are some practical ways you can help your children make wise choices about the parties that they attend?

## Additional Resources

If you are interested in further reading on this subject, these resources may be helpful.

### For Parents

*Parenting Teens with Love and Logic* by Foster Cline and Jim Fay

*Pure Pleasure: Why Do Christians Feel So Bad About Feeling Good?* by Gary Thomas

*Why Christian Kids Rebel* by Tim Kimmel

# 3

# Divorce

## Paul Basden

I will never forget Friday night, March 20, 2015. Our church was sponsoring a marriage conference, and the opening session was a surprise celebration. I had the privilege of presiding over a wedding ceremony for Phil and Jessica. What made it so unusual was that this was their second marriage...to each other. Here is what I said to everyone as I set up the surprise.

> Tonight is a night we will never forget. Jessica and Phil got married nine years ago, but they faced troubles from the very beginning—in-laws, finances, communication... your typical marital minefields. Unfortunately, they didn't know how to deal with these problems.
>
> She got hurt, and he got angry. Actually, they were both hurt. Phil later acknowledged, "Anger is a guy's way of being hurt." The pain caused by their incompetence to solve their problems led to separation. But that solution didn't sit well with either of them. They still cared about each other and couldn't bear the idea of being apart permanently. So they moved in and moved out, hung in and

fell out, living in the ambivalence of an on-again, off-again marriage.

After several years of this unhealthy holding pattern, they finally decided to divorce. They simply couldn't come up with a better solution. Sadly, they were egged on by friends and family to call it quits. So they formally and legally ended their marriage. They were finally divorced.

Yet that decision seemed so once and for all, they couldn't swallow it. So in time they began dating. Again.

One evening they got together to watch a few movies from the local video store. One of the films, *Fireproof*, was the story of a firefighter who was losing his marriage but who by God's grace found full restoration with his wife. As they watched the film, for the first time, Phil and Jessica didn't feel alone. For the first time, they felt like they understood anger. For the first time, they felt like God was with them.

They began to talk about restoring their marriage. They decided that if their relationship was going to work, it needed to have a change of scenery. So they left family, friends, and familiar surroundings and moved halfway across the country to Frisco, Texas, where they found Preston Trail Community Church. When they heard about our marriage ministry called ReEngage, they jumped right in and joined a group of couples where they could focus on how to have a Christ-centered marriage.

Guess what? They have decided to remarry! Guess what else? Tonight we get to witness their wedding! They are officially and legally exchanging vows in just a few minutes, and you and I are their witnesses. I told you it's a night we'll never forget!

## Divorce in Your Kids' World

If every unhappy marriage had this kind of happy ending, a chapter on divorce would be unnecessary. But we all know this is not the norm. Divorce is a constant companion in our culture. Even our children know it. As much as parents try to protect kids from the after-effects of divorce, it's impossible to shelter them from the unintended consequences of a failed marriage.

Talking to children about divorce was hardly necessary sixty years ago. In 1957, only one state offered no-fault divorce; by 1995, all 50 states did. Given this reality, your children need you to engage them in conversations about this sensitive subject. They probably have friends whose parents are divorced. Someone in their extended family may have experienced divorce—maybe even one or both of their own parents (you).

There are two things *not* to say when this topic comes up.

1. "Divorce is the worst thing that can ever happen—maybe even an unforgivable sin."
2. "Divorce is not all that bad. The problem is with marriage, which may be outdated in today's world."

If those are the wrong things to say, what are the right things to say? What *do* you tell your kids about divorce?

## Divorce Is Not God's Ideal

Tell them it is not God's original plan for a man and woman to vow they will spend a lifetime together, only to seek a divorce later. Explain that God did not design a man and woman to become one in marriage and then divide back into two. God intended two to become one and to live a lifetime of faithfulness to one another. As the creation story states so beautifully, "This explains why a man leaves his father and mother and is joined to his wife, and the two are united into one" (Genesis 2:24 NLT).

The first book in the Old Testament celebrates the union of man and woman, and the last book in the Old Testament protests the dissolution of that union. God, speaking through the prophet Malachi, said to Israel, "I hate divorce!" (Malachi 2:16 NLT).

That's strong language, to say God hates something. Does God really hate anything?

Yes, God hates anything that harms his human creatures and undercuts his character. That's why God hates divorce—because of its consequences.

A minister to single adults at a large church asked those in his ministry to answer a question: "In one sentence or paragraph, why do you think God hates divorce?" Here are some of the answers 500 divorced parents wrote down.

1. It's never over for anyone completely.
2. It devastates families.
3. God sees in graphic detail our losses and pain.
4. It makes people wonder if being a Christian makes any difference.
5. It breaks up families for generations to come.
6. Children are denied a normal childhood.
7. God knows and feels our total despair and emptiness. His heart of love grieves for his children.
8. Divorce leaves a family in a state of insecurity and confusion.
9. Raising children separately is just not the way God intended it.
10. The children's loyalties are torn between the two people they love most.[1]

I don't recommend using the word "hate" when you tell your young child what God thinks about divorce, but I do warn you against papering over the pain divorce brings—pain to the couple as well as pain to the children.

However, your goal is not simply to say God's ideal is not divorce. Your aim is to tell your children God's ideal is for married people to stay married. Hopefully you can steer the conversation into an insightful discussion about the meaning of marriage from a biblical perspective. And you can start with Jesus.

Jesus is abundantly clear about the purpose and permanence of marriage. In Matthew's Gospel, we read a story of his encounter with the religious experts of his day.

> Some Pharisees came and tried to trap him with this question: "Should a man be allowed to divorce his wife for just any reason?"
>
> "Haven't you read the Scriptures?" Jesus replied. "They record that from the beginning 'God made them male and female.'" And he said, "'This explains why a man leaves his father and mother and is joined to his wife, and the two are united into one.' Since they are no longer two but one, let no one split apart what God has joined together" (Matthew 19:3-6 NLT).

Using this Scripture, you can highlight three important things with your children.

First, tell them marriage means "you first." When Jesus said "a man leaves his father and mother," he was pointing out that marriage creates a new priority—one's spouse. Prior to marriage, any number of people or things could be first in your life.

- your parents, who conceived you, provided for you, and raised you
- your freewheeling single lifestyle, which afforded little accountability, lots of adaptability, and almost endless flexibility
- your many romantic interests, which underlined your freedom to "play the field" rather than be tied down

Prior to marriage, any of these could be priority one. But at the wedding altar, all that changes. Standing in front of family and friends and saying "I do" to another person means you are saying "I don't" to anyone or anything else that once claimed your heart's allegiance. Marriage means "you first."

Then tell your kids marriage means "you only." The phrase "the two are united into one" points to a permanent bond that is not easily dissolved. "United" can also be translated "cleave"—which can mean to hold on to a person without letting go or to glue two objects together so they are inseparable. The word is also used in the Bible to describe skin clinging to bone and scales clinging to fish. Add this up, and you get the picture of a permanent bond. God intended a marital union to be exclusive. Marriage means "you only."

Finally, tell them marriage means "you always." Jesus took marriage so seriously that he warned, "Let no one split apart what God has joined together." God planned for marriage to be a permanent covenant—not a handshake deal that you can walk away from or a business contract that can be canceled when terms are not met. God's ideal is a lifelong union of two imperfect persons, held together by grace. Marriage means "you always."

I have officiated at dozens of weddings, and every couple whose service I performed dreamed of a happy marriage. They wanted a marriage that could be described as "you first, you only, and you always." I have also counseled many couples who ended up getting divorced, and every one of them wished their relationship had been strong enough to go the distance. Nobody who gets married plans for a divorce. Even when there are extenuating circumstances, couples know that divorce is not God's ideal. Tell that to your children when the "D-word" discussion comes up. Help them understand that God wants strong, healthy marriages—including theirs one day.

## It's Not Their Fault

Divorce is never a child's fault. There are many reasons couples choose to divorce, but it is always a decision made solely by adults. Make sure your children hear you say, "Kids don't cause divorce."

To better understand the causes of divorce, look at the next few verses in Matthew 19.

> "Then why did Moses say in the law that a man could give
> his wife a written notice of divorce and send her away?"
> they asked.

> Jesus replied, "Moses permitted divorce only as a con-
> cession to your hard hearts, but it was not what God had
> originally intended. And I tell you this, whoever divorces
> his wife and marries someone else commits adultery—
> unless his wife has been unfaithful" (Matthew 19:7-9 NLT).

Jesus simplified the collapse of modern marriage with one eternal insight: A hard heart causes divorce. But who is surprised? Isn't hardness of heart the cause of all sin?

In marriage, hardness of heart takes many forms. At the top of the list is adultery. Whether it is spurred on by online sexual excitement or real-life sexual opportunity, adultery is everywhere. Whether it begins with a Facebook friend request or a happy hour come-on, adultery is an exercise in betrayal and deceit. Whether it is motivated by anger at one's spouse or fear of one's own aging, adultery harms everyone dear to you. Your spouse feels rejected, your children feel insecure, your friends feel confused, another family may feel anger toward you, you may come to hate yourself, and you may feel like God is finished with you. The consequences are staggering.

You may not want to talk to younger children about adultery, but your older children need to hear about it from you—if only to correct the misinformation they are hearing at school and seeing onscreen. Our media portrays adultery as exciting and inviting. Cut through the Hollywood lies to tell your kids the truth.

Are there other causes of divorce you should talk to your kids about? Probably. The list is long: physical and verbal abuse, apathy, money issues, sexual expectations, relational blind spots, spiritual immaturity, emotional toxicity, communication ignorance, anger mismanagement, keeping up with the neighbors...and the beat goes on.

As you engage your children in age-appropriate conversations about what can cause divorce, remember these wise words from Rudolf Dreikurs in a book by John Claypool, one of my ministerial mentors: "Children are keen observers but poor interpreters."[2] That is, they see everything but can't understand what they are seeing. When they see their parents fighting or stonewalling, they feel the tension—but they think they caused it. They add two plus two but get twelve. Instead of understanding that it's not their fault, they often think "I must have done something wrong" or "I can fix it." As an adult, you must tell them it's not their fault, they did nothing wrong, and they can't fix it.

It would be great if this kind of conversation (and so many others in this book) could be one and done—you tell them once, and your job is finished. You do it right, and they will remember for life. But that's a pipe dream. Children who have experienced divorce, whether directly or indirectly, reach wrong conclusions and harbor illogical thoughts because of the power of their emotions. The world feels uncertain and unpredictable. Life feels sad and lonely. They feel powerless to make their dreams of family harmony come true. That's why you may need to tell your children over and over that divorce is not their fault.

## It's Not the End of the World for Parents

To start with, kids need to hear that divorce is not the end of the world for their parents. They may easily conclude that Mom and Dad will always have a troubled relationship and will never like each other again, even as friends. In their simple way of thinking, two people who once loved each other should be able to get along.

Remember that divorce carries with it some problems that can be solved and also some tensions that can only be managed. Assure your kids that adults who divorce can indeed go on to live productive lives as single parents or with a new marriage partner. If one of those examples reflects your situation, tell your kids your story. Keep the details age-appropriate, and never throw your ex-spouse under the bus. But let your children know that God has forgiven you for your role in your marriage breakup, that you are working on having a good relationship with your ex, and that your life is meaningful on this side of divorce.

If your child is old enough to understand deeper biblical truths, consider walking them through Jesus's teaching in Matthew 12 on the unforgivable sin…and assure them that Jesus is not referring to divorce. You could say something like this.

> One day Jesus healed a person by removing a disturbed spirit from his life. The onlookers thought that anyone who had that kind of authority over illness must be filled with God's power. But the religious leaders disagreed. They mocked Jesus, saying that his power could come only from Satan, because only evil Satan would have the power to cast out evil spirits. Jesus told them who was wrong and who was right.
>
> > "If Satan is casting out Satan, he is divided and fighting against himself. His own kingdom will not survive. So I tell you, every sin and blasphemy can be forgiven—except blasphemy against the Holy Spirit, which will never be forgiven. Anyone who speaks against the Son of Man can be forgiven, but anyone who speaks against the Holy Spirit will never be forgiven, either in this world or in the world to come" (Matthew 12:26,31-32 NLT).
>
> What he meant was this: Two groups of people saw one man do the same miracle. One group concluded God was acting through Jesus, but the other group refused to see God acting through Jesus. So Jesus said that the second group had committed the unforgivable sin. That is, the only sin that can't be forgiven is the sin of denying that God is at work in Jesus. He called it "blasphemy against the Holy Spirit" because it ignores and rejects the power of God's Spirit working in Jesus. It is unforgivable because it

turns away from the only source of forgiveness available—God's love in Christ. This means that all other sins can be forgiven, including divorce.

Divorce is not the last word for parents. God still has a purpose for every parent who humbly bows before him. God specializes in giving second chances. Divorce does not automatically disqualify someone from experiencing God's love and serving in God's kingdom. If God could forgive Moses for murder, David for adultery, and Simon Peter for cowardice, then God can offer forgiveness to any adult who has gone through divorce—if he or she truly seeks it.

This is certainly true for a friend of mine whose wife left him while he was studying at seminary to become a minister. She wanted an acting career, so she moved to the West Coast to seek fame and fortune. She left behind a man with a broken heart and an overwhelming feeling that he was a failure. His despair was so deep, his physician placed him on a suicide watch. He decided to drop out of seminary in hopes of reconstructing his life. He went into the family business and served in his church, but he couldn't escape the haunting questions that swirled in his head every day. Had he committed the unforgivable sin? Was her exit somehow his fault? Could he have prevented her from leaving if he had been a better husband? Would a church ever want him on staff now that he was divorced? Could God ever use him again? How long would it take the Lord to answer his perpetual prayer, "Restore to me the joy of your salvation" (Psalm 51:12 NLT)?

These questions troubled him for several years until one day God providentially arranged for him to meet a young woman who saw him not as a divorced man, but as a man who loved Jesus and who loved her. They fell in love, grew in love, and finally vowed their love in marriage. He returned to church ministry and has been welcomed at every turn by people who know that God still has a purpose for anyone who humbly bows before him. God specializes in giving second chances. Tell your children that divorce is not the end of the world for parents.

## It's Not the End of the World for Kids

Also tell your children that divorce is not the end of the world for kids. This is especially important if your children are splitting time between two divorced parents and wishing they could be a "normal family" again. Kids who are being parented by a dad and mom living in separate locations need hope that the stress of divorce is not the final word.

The first time I saw a child survive and thrive in a divorce, the parents determined it would be so. They were friends of mine, and they had one son. He was a preschooler when the divorce occurred. Despite the less-than-ideal world they created by ending their marriage, both Mom and Dad decided—for the sake of their son—never to feud or fight. Instead of using him as a pawn in their game of getting even, they loved him as a son who deserved their best efforts at living in peace. As their son grew older, I noticed that he exhibited no unusual signs of insecurity or abandonment or family dysfunction. Instead, he developed into a young man who loved both parents, made wise decisions, and was well-adjusted in life. Stories like this are legion. Kids need to know they can survive this ordeal—and even thrive.

I am not able to prove this biblically, but I believe children affected by divorce have a special place in God's heart. I can't find a Bible verse that affirms this idea, but I can get close. Often in Scripture, God pledged to care for orphans and widows in Israel—people who were distressed and disadvantaged in that patriarchal culture. For example, in Psalm 68:5 we read, "A father to the fatherless, a defender of widows, is God in his holy dwelling."

Children of divorce are not literally fatherless or motherless, but I believe God cares for them in a similar way. I think God recognizes that they need both a father's love and a mother's love to develop into emotionally healthy adults. And in the turbulence of divorce, when a child does not have access to both parents 24/7, God is prepared to step into the picture and breathe his peace into the family unrest.

When I was a young Christian, one of my favorite hymns was "Dear Lord and Father of Mankind." One verse always caught my attention and quickened my prayers. It captures what God longs to do for children of divorce.

> Drop Thy still dews of quietness,
> Till all our strivings cease;
> Take from our souls the strain and stress,
> And let our ordered lives confess
> The beauty of Thy peace.[3]

### It's Not the End of the World for the Family

Finally, encourage your kids by emphasizing that divorce is not the end of the world for the family. The family will look different—birth parents will no longer be living together under one roof with their children. But God redeems families! God can bring long-term healing to single-parent families and blended families.

I've had the privilege of watching several single mothers and single fathers raise their children in homes that were havens of happiness and wholeness. One of these women went through a divorce when her two sons were young. Her husband was the primary breadwinner. When the marriage ended, she was faced with two harsh realities: She had to find a full-time job that would support her family of three, and she had to become the primary caregiver for her two little boys. By God's grace, she has succeeded beautifully.

For more than a decade I've watched her make wise decisions about offering age-appropriate freedoms to her sons. She has customized her parenting for two boys with very different temperaments. She has raised them in church without forcing them to accept her religious beliefs. All in all, these boys have matured into responsible young men while living in a single-parent household. Their family is intact and healthy despite the difficulties of divorce.

Several years ago I performed a wedding for a couple whose new marriage would create a blended family—two children from her first marriage and three from his. The service included all the kids in the "unity sand ceremony." Here is how it worked. Near the end of the service, the bride's children walked to a table and poured sand of one color into a unity vase; then the groom's children poured sand of a different color into the same vase. The union of two differently colored sands pointed to the unity of two formerly different and distinct families. It was a visual representation of two family units becoming one, showing that their marriage was more than just the union of two individuals—it was the creation of a new family. The exchange of wedding rings showed the unity of husband and wife, and the unity sand ceremony showed the unity of the new blended family.

That simple act in their wedding ceremony was part of a larger pattern of intentional parenting that this husband and wife have practiced in their new expanded family. In fact, I would say a spirit of oneness exists in this blended family that would be the envy of any mom and dad raising their biological children. Divorce did not spell disaster for these two families that are now one.

## Conclusion

When opportunities arise for you to talk to your kids about divorce, tell them that it is not God's ideal. There is no need to berate yourself if you've been through a divorce, but your children need to know how God envisions marriage. Take the time to describe a healthy Christ-centered marriage so they have that image in their minds as they mature. Also tell them that divorce is never the children's fault. It's an adult decision with repercussions for the kids, but no child has the power to cause or prevent divorce. Finally, tell them that divorce is not the end of the world—for the child, for the parents, or for the family. As you share these truths, you will give your children grace-filled wisdom for navigating the ins and outs of living in a single-parent family or a blended family. By modeling and teaching them that God is always present, you will have the joy of pointing them to the Lord, who keeps his divine promise: "God is our refuge and strength, always ready to help in times of trouble" (Psalm 46:1 NLT).

........................................................................................

*Dear Lord,*

*Divorce is so much a part of our culture, everyone seems to be affected. When our kids feel the impact, we want to help. We want to assure them that you are near, that your purpose for us has not suddenly ended, and that your love can mend us and heal us and give us hope. When you open the door for these conversations, give us courage to enter in and wisdom to speak the truth in love, knowing that anything less will neither honor you nor truly help our children. Thank you for second chances.*

*Amen.*

## Breaking It Down for Every Age

Although divorce is not a simple topic for any thoughtful parent to discuss with their child, it is particularly painful if you are talking about the dissolution of your own marriage. If you are facing divorce or walking through its painful aftermath, we recommend that you consider helping your child process his questions with the assistance of a professional Christian counselor. Whether you are dealing with divorce in theory or on a more personal level, however, there are a few important talking points to keep in mind at various phases of your child's development.

## Elementary-Aged Kids

As we mentioned earlier, kids are keen observers but poor inter-preters. Therefore, it is perhaps most important with younger children to start with the statement that *divorce is an adult decision, that kids are never at fault, and that they have no power to change the outcome.* As you talk to your kids, acknowledge the deep hurt that divorce causes for all who are involved, and encourage your child to verbalize the sadness or pain she is feeling. Remember that kids feel sad not only about their own situations but also when their friends are having a tough time.

When younger kids ask why in regard to divorce, shield them from details that are too weighty for them to bear. But as we have seen, you can talk to them about the hardness of the human heart that leads us to sin. Help them understand that our sin always hurts God and ourselves, and it often hurts other people too. But go on to explain that divorce is not an unforgivable sin. Reassure them that God can bring healing, even from the pain of divorce.

## Tweens

As your child reaches the tween years, it may be helpful to answer his questions about divorce by also clarifying God's purpose for marriage. Help him understand that God created marriage to signify "you first," "you only," and "you always" in terms of your relationship with your spouse. Be mindful that popular culture is sending your tween a steady stream of messages that run counter to God's vision for marriage. Take advantage of the opportunity presented by songs, movies, books, or TV shows to talk about what marriage is meant to be and why marriage so often fails. If your tween has been personally impacted by divorce, continue assuring him that there was nothing he could have done differently to prevent it or to change that outcome.

## Teens

Your teen's view of marriage may become jaded during this season of life because of personal experiences, friends' struggles, and cultural messages. On the opposite extreme, she may succumb to a highly romanticized notion of marriage, placing her hope in a soul mate who will one day complete her life. If you are married, one of the best ways to help your teen capture a vision for a healthy, authentic, flawed, and yet Christ-centered marriage is to model it in your own home. Whether you are married or divorced, discuss with your teen in an honest and age-appropriate way the challenges you've faced, the lessons you've learned, and especially the ways you've seen God redeem your own seasons of relational hardship or brokenness.

## Questions for Personal Reflection or Group Discussion

1. How much have you told your child about God's intent for marriage?
2. What do you think your child understands about divorce?
3. What worries you most about talking to your child about divorce?
4. How has divorce affected you? Your spouse? Your child?
5. Where do you most need God's healing touch on the subject of divorce?

## Additional Resources

If you are interested in further reading on this subject, these resources may be helpful.

## For Parents

*Broken: Making Sense of Life After Your Parents' Divorce* by Tim Baker

*Helping Children Survive Divorce* by Archibald D. Hart

*Saving Your Second Marriage Before It Starts* by Les and Leslie Parrott

*The Divorce Decision* by Gary Richmond

*The Heart of Remarriage* by Gary Smalley and Greg Smalley

# 4

# Having Sex

### Jim Johnson

Nothing can trigger the parental fight-or-flight response like the prospect of having "the talk." The first attempt in our household certainly didn't go as expected, and it wasn't planned either. Our oldest, Ben, was nine at the time and had not shown much interest in the topic. One fateful evening, I put him to bed with our nightly ritual and closed the door behind me as he teetered on the cusp of dreamland.

Unbeknownst to me at the time, my wife, Robin, was watching a PBS documentary in the den. The subject was how and when to talk with your children about sex. As I walked out of Ben's bedroom, she met me in the hallway with a panicked look on her face and an urgent question: "Have you had 'the talk' with Ben yet?"

"He really hasn't been asking," I stammered, somewhat taken aback by her out-of-the-blue concern. "So, no, I haven't." Given the new information Robin had just acquired courtesy of PBS, this clearly wasn't the correct answer.

She hurriedly relayed to me the content of the studies cited in the documentary, which had determined that by the time a child is nine, you have already missed the boat on having "the talk."

"So you need to go back in there and tell him right now," she asserted.

"Honey, I'm not going to wake him up to have that conversation with him now. But if you think it's that important, feel free to go ahead and talk to him yourself."

I had never seen Robin quite this passionate about a parental issue, but I knew enough to understand that it would be in everyone's best interests if she were able to act on it. As I stepped aside, she opened the door to Ben's room and gently sat down beside him on the bed. Putting her hand on his shoulder, she said, "Ben...Ben, wake up. I need to talk with you about something."

"Whaaat?" Ben muttered as he slowly regained consciousness.

"I need to talk with you about something very important," my wife responded. Clearing her throat, she said, "I want to talk to you about the facts of life."

"Oh, Mom, I already know the facts of life," Ben replied, still wiping sleep from his eyes.

Clearly surprised, Robin said, "Really? Well, tell me what you know."

With a voice that held the conviction of one who knows what he's talking about, Ben said, "Life is tough, but you've got to keep trying."

With that, Robin cleared her throat and sheepishly intoned, "You are exactly right, honey. You go on back to sleep, and I'll see you in the morning." And that was the last time Robin had "the talk" with any of our boys.

I was happy to take over the educational process from there, and as our three sons' sexual curiosity developed to the point of asking questions, I think they were all relieved that I was the designated instructor for this valuable life lesson.

Well, if nine was too late to have the talk back then, we might all be shocked to discover what the prescribed age to start having intentional and thoughtful conversations with our children is now! Children are increasingly bombarded by images and messages about sex.

One source asserts that between music videos, television, movies, and the internet, our children receive 14,000 messages with some sexual content every year![1] This likely explains why, as studies show, children are becoming sexually active at an early age.

To complicate matters, young adults are postponing relational commitment and are choosing to marry at a later age. By comparison, in the New Testament era, it was not unusual for adolescents to marry as young as 12 to 15 years of age. Today, the average age of a groom in the United States is 29 years. The average age of a bride is 27.[2] When you do the math, young adults who have a Christian commitment are forced to deal with the spiritual struggle of living out their sexuality faithfully for an additional 15 years in a highly sex-charged culture. Not an easy task for sure, and statistics reveal that a significant number of them have simply given up the fight.[3]

In addition, the current generation of parents grew up after the sexual revolution of the '60s. As a result, parental perspectives on this issue abound. Some think it's not a huge concern for their kids to be sexually active if they take precautions. Other parents have unresolved issues of guilt and shame lingering from their own sexual stories. You do not have to observe our culture very long to realize that there is no longer a monolithic sexual ethic that provides a moral foundation for our children. Most troubling is that sex is now being disconnected from the context of a meaningful relationship. Although it is frightening to consider, we are watching a generation grow up whose first experience with sex was a party game.

But what about kids raised in church? Unfortunately, the statistics among professing Christians aren't very encouraging either. A recent study found that 80 percent of unmarried Christians age 19 and older said they have had sex. Seventy percent of those kids had been sexually active in the previous year.[4] Clearly, the biblical teaching that ultimate intimacy is reserved for ultimate commitment is becoming increasingly irrelevant to those both inside and outside the walls of the church.

It's no wonder communicating with our kids about God's design for sex feels like a monumental challenge. Not only do we have to talk about the awkward details of the act itself, but we feel compelled to convince them they should follow God's way of enjoying this amazing gift even though the tides of culture and their own hormones are flowing powerfully against them. I think we would all agree this part of parenting is hard, but it is not hopeless. With God's Word to guide us and the courage to think in some new ways, you can communicate truths and principles that will protect and bless your children and give them the best chance of having the marriage, and the intimate life within marriage, you want them to enjoy.

What can you tell your kids about having sex? I would like to articulate three biblical principles that are simple but not simplistic. These truths will help you communicate to your children God's will and purpose for sexual intimacy. Following these principles, I will lay out some practical ideas you can give them that will help them live a life counter to the culture.

## God's Good Gift for Married People

In Genesis 1, God sings a recurring refrain over his budding creation: "It is good!" From stars to planets, moose to marsupials, sea bass to sharks, pine trees to petunias, man to woman, it's all good. They all fulfill God's creative purpose of voicing his delight, joy, and life in a material expression of his true character. The focus of his creation, however, is the creature who bears his image in a unique way. This creature, in two forms, male and female, is given the blessed task of multiplying, filling the earth, and managing it for God's sake. From the very beginning, the intimate act of procreation was deemed good.

In Genesis 2, Adam joins God's refrain when he sees Eve. After walking through a zoological inventory with God and helping classify his handiwork, it becomes apparent to both that Adam has been left somewhat out in the cold with regard to a true companion. "Not good" was an unacceptable refrain for God. So he puts

Adam down for a nap, and in a final flair of creativity, God forms Eve. When Adam awakens, he is breathless as he gazes at her, and in an early Hebrew dialect, he cries out something to the effect of "Whoa, man!" You can read the official announcement in Genesis 2:23. Even though Adam doesn't say the exact words, he clearly is singing, "This is good…this is very good."

From there the story goes on to declare, "That is why a man leaves his father and mother and is united to his wife, and they become one flesh. Adam and his wife were both naked, and they felt no shame" (Genesis 2:24-25). The phrase "and they become one flesh" is the Old Testament way of talking about sexual intercourse. It is the culminating gift God gives his beloved creatures so they can experience divinely inspired intimacy. Unfortunately, throughout much of Christian history, some believers have viewed and written about sex as if it were dirty, unholy, and something to be engaged in only for procreation. Thankfully, the teaching that sex is God's good gift for married people has reemerged in our day.

This is the first principle to share as you carefully build the foundation for your child's thinking about sex. The obvious task is to communicate the God-givenness of sex in teachable moments. Oftentimes, though, our children hear the opposite message through our offhand comments about sex or our reactions to sexual content in media. If we're not careful, we can send judgmental messages about a real-life situation or a scene we are viewing. As a result, our children may draw the conclusion that all sex is shameful, simply because they can't process the nuances of that particular situation.

We can also communicate the goodness of sex when our children start discovering the pleasurable sensations of their own sexual organs. As nature would have it, kids have no inbred understanding about where and when it is appropriate to touch themselves (insert your own embarrassing story here). Unfortunately, the Bible is silent on this sensitive topic and offers no guidance. So in the absence of any biblical admonition, I cautiously offer some wisdom gleaned from raising three boys.

The theme of privacy served us well in explaining several sexual issues. As we helped our boys understand that they have "private parts" that no one has the right to touch, it easily followed that they should only touch themselves when they are in private. This approach will help you avoid public embarrassment, but it doesn't address the need for ongoing conversations about masturbation when your kids reach puberty. The best idea may simply be not to freak out. That will go a long way in helping your kids avoid attaching shame to the natural curiosity every child has about discovering the wonders of their bodies. Needless to say, how we guide them and how we speak of these particular actions is going to leave a lasting imprint on what they feel about their sexuality.

Another teachable opportunity presents itself when his natural curiosity about the opposite sex begins to emerge. You may find him searching the internet to find pictures or get answers to his questions. A knee-jerk, harsh, and shaming response may help quash the fear that our child has now discovered pornography, but such a response might leave an indelible impression that sex is bad or that he needs to be secretive or untruthful in searching out answers to his curiosity.

Simple and thoughtful questions like "Honey, what's going on inside your head and heart that made you want to look at these pictures?" will help you discern what is truly driving this behavior. If you discern that it is indeed a natural curiosity, then you can begin to go through age-appropriate resources to help answer her questions and thereby continue to build a healthy sexual foundation that will serve her well into her future.

## The Blessing of Using Sex God's Way

I want to return to Genesis 2 because, as simple as it sounds, it is incredibly profound. It describes the state of married life: "That is why a man leaves his father and mother and is united to his wife, and they become one flesh." This is God's relational order. This is the way you and I are wired to be intimately related to another human being.

## Leaving

First, we must leave something. In the original setting, it literally meant to move out of your parents' tent. The point is not so much geographical as it is relational. God, in his wisdom, is telling us to cut the ties of emotional dependence on our parents.

Why is this so important? As a kid, when you skinned your knee, you ran to your parents. When you broke up with your boyfriend, you turned to Mom or Dad for counsel and comfort, and you learned to depend on them. They were your source of help, comfort, and support.

For the marriage relationship to grow, however, those earlier emotional ties must be cut. The writer of Genesis is declaring that when you get married, you and your spouse are to turn to each other for those emotional resources. Depending on each other instead of your parents in times of trouble and pain creates a deep bond. Many young couples ignore this command—and consequently struggle with in-law problems. Marriage is meant for two, not two plus a mom or dad. Adjusting to married life is hard enough without complicating the process by allowing others with their own agendas into the marital mix.

Along with cutting ties of dependence, it's also important to identify some of the dysfunctional relational patterns we learn in our families of origin and carry into marriage. Unless we determine to leave these unhealthy habits behind, we are bound to repeat them. The conventional wisdom is that two "half people" will make a whole marriage. The truth is, it takes two whole people to make one great marriage!

## Uniting

Second, the text says you must be united together. You may recall that in biblical times, marriages were arranged. Couples didn't marry for love as we do today. Often, the marriages were arranged for political or financial reasons—thus the need for a period of betrothal. A betrothal provided the time and opportunity for the future husband and wife to get to know one another, to spend time together, to eat together, to begin a friendship, and to have time to build a relationship without the complications of sex.

In Judaism, the period of sexual abstinence during the betrothal gave the couple much to look forward to after their wedding. When the ceremony was over, the couple would go into a private room to consecrate their vows through the act of sexual intercourse while everyone else stood around waiting for the buffet line to open. It was a big deal because now they were fulfilling Genesis 2:24-25. They were becoming fully and completely one.

This scenario is God's order lived out. The good news is that when you do life and relationships God's way, you will experience the full blessing he had in mind when he created marriage. Done his way, you don't bring unwanted disruption and dysfunction into the marriage. In other words, you create a healthy relational environment that gives you the best possible chance to enjoy the intimate life God has in mind for you. It's important for our kids to understand that when you do sex God's way, you will be blessed.

## Misuse the Gift, Miss the Blessing

This Genesis text is all about the idea of order. In our culture, when couples start dating, sex is expected early in the relationship. This expectation may seem exciting and fun, but another dynamic is at work here. Having sex can quickly get in the way of developing a healthy, mutually beneficial relationship. Sexual liaisons early in a couple's relationship can dominate the time and energy devoted to the relationship. As a result, the couple doesn't spend enough time cutting the ties of emotional dependence on parents and creating new bonds with one another. It also becomes more difficult to do the hard work of processing and resolving the unhealthy dynamics of past relationships. In effect, misusing sex in a relationship circumvents the opportunity to become relationally whole before entering into a marriage covenant.

In a similar vein, as sex dominates a couple's early life together, they often struggle to make time to truly get to know one another, grow their relationship emotionally and spiritually, and simply learn to be friends. When the sex cools down, what is often left is two people who have used each other sexually but have no real friendship to speak of, and the relationship simply dissolves. The sad irony is this: Sexual intimacy was given by God to bond and complete a couple in marriage, but when it is misused, it can lead to the relationship's demise. Things work a certain way, and when you get matters of the heart and body out of order, you will miss much of the blessing God has in mind for you.

## Helping Your Child Make Wise Choices About Sex

God's design for having sex can be summed up in a simple principle: Ultimate sexual intimacy is reserved for those who make the ultimate covenant commitment to each other in marriage. Certainly, this is the place to begin. But when it comes to something as powerful as the human sexual drive, coupled with romantic love, information alone rarely matches the hormonal urges adolescents and young adults face. They need additional guidance to have the best opportunity to experience the divine gift of intimacy as God intended. Communicating content alone will fail. They need a commensurate effort to develop their character. Here are some practical steps you can take to equip your kids to make wise sexual decisions.

*Reframe your goal for your child's future intimate life.*

A good goal: Help my children keep their "true love waits" pledges.

In most quarters of conservative Christianity, the primary goal of parenting, with respect to having sex, is to get children to their wedding nights with their virginity intact. The True Love Waits campaign, which has made its way across the country to the youth groups of numerous evangelical churches, is an example of this sentiment. This is a worthy goal, but I would like to suggest that given the realities of our current situation, it is no longer adequate. Here's why.

First, this goal is shortsighted. If the goal is simply to hold on to one's virginity until the wedding night, a simpler approach would be to return to the medieval custom of the chastity belt. No muss, maybe some fuss. Or we can demonize sex so strongly that our children will buy the lie that sex is dirty and is only for procreation.

I think we all want much more for our children than this. We want our children to have such a trustworthy relationship with God that their strongest desire is to honor him with their bodies and trust his Word on this deeply personal issue. We want them to understand and know how to have an intimate and faithful relationship with another person over a lifetime. A goal of saving sex for marriage, while noble, can't guarantee this. And sometimes the methods parents choose are detrimental to this larger goal.

Second, the strict insistence on abstinence has led many adolescents to question what constitutes virginity. Does one lose it by participating in oral sex? Anal sex? Most Christian kids are not asking "How can I honor God with my body?" but "How far can I go and still be considered a virgin?" Ironically, the quest to keep our kids' virginity intact may push them toward more varied and dangerous sexual activities.

And third, a goal of saving sex for marriage is based on all-or-nothing thinking, which sets many of our children up to fail—about eight out of ten of them if the surveys are accurate. What happens in the hearts of our children when one night their adolescent curiosity or passion overwhelms them and they go all the way? Simply put, they have failed. Their purity, in their minds, is forever tainted. They feel like they've truly blown it. And if you find out, you likely feel devastated.

How will they respond? Kids typically react to this experience in one of three ways. Those with a strong faith may own up to knowingly going against God's will and genuinely repent and make a renewed commitment to honor God in their relationships going forward. Other teens or young adults with a spiritual background may become so overwhelmed with shame and guilt that they feel unworthy to approach God. They may hesitate to go back to church for fear they will be judged or ostracized. Taken together, these sentiments can become a significant stumbling block to their future spiritual growth. Frankly, I think this is one of the primary reasons most kids who grow up in church drift away in their college years. They simply don't know how to handle the guilt, the shame, and the cognitive dissonance between what their faith tells them and what they are practicing. So they just drop out.

Finally, some will say, "Well, I'm not a virgin anymore. I've blown it. Besides, it was exciting and wonderful, and nothing really happened, so why shouldn't I keep having sex?" In their minds, there's no reason not to have sex, and the road to promiscuity beckons. This is the danger of all-or-nothing thinking. It paints our kids into spiritual corners from which they often can't escape.

> A better goal: Help my children get to the altar as sexually whole humans by helping them learn and practice the virtue of chastity.

I want to challenge you to reframe your goal for your children's sexual choices. Instead of simply trying to get your children to the altar as virgins, set a goal to get your children to the altar as sexually whole people. At first this may sound redundant, but there is a subtle and powerful difference between these goals. To do this, you will need to espouse and encourage your child to practice the virtue of chastity. Ugh…I know this sounds hopelessly out-of-date, but hang with me as I try to reclaim this dusty but profound word.

Chastity is a classical and biblical virtue that certainly has sexual connotations, but at its heart, it's about remaining faithful to one's covenant commitments. If a believer is not married, then his or her covenant with God is to remain celibate until entering into marriage. The apostle Paul sets out this boundary for us in 1 Corinthians 6:18-20.

> Flee from sexual immorality. All other sins a person commits are outside the body, but whoever sins sexually, sins against their own body. Do you not know that your bodies are temples of the Holy Spirit, who is in you, whom you have received from God? You are not your own; you were bought at a price. Therefore honor God with your bodies.

Those who are married practice chastity by honoring and keeping the vows of sexual fidelity they made to their spouses. The writer of Hebrews provides clarity for us on this point: "Give honor to marriage, and remain faithful to one another in marriage. God will surely judge people who are immoral and those who commit adultery" (Hebrews 13:4 NLT).

With this small reframing, your goal becomes far more than just getting your kids to the altar with their virginity intact. Instead, it focuses your efforts on helping them grow into individuals who know how to live faithfully in a real-life covenant relationship. This knowledge and skill will be essential for them to experience true sexual intimacy and marital fulfillment. The difference between these goals is that one is focused on a single event in time, while the other is focused on helping them develop spiritually based relational habits that will last a lifetime. This not only is a more holistic approach but also creates a relational environment that will keep your children's hearts open to your guidance while they are learning this important value.

If you focus on teaching and leading your children to develop a virtue, you won't be surprised when your kids make mistakes and poor decisions along the way. You'll also incorporate your kids into the learning process. Here's a thought I'd like for you to ponder. When it comes to the value of honesty, did your kids learn how to practice it perfectly the first time you taught it to them? Of course not. There were probably periods in their development when they really struggled with learning to tell the truth.

Our youngest son, Brady, struggled with this a bit. Evidently, he liked to tell "stories." It became so widely known at his school that on one occasion, Robin heard from another mom whose child was in his class that when her little one came home from school and told her something a bit fanciful, she would say, "Now, is that the truth, or is that a Brady tale?" Okay, I admit, he may have been in the "slow group" when it came to learning this value. But as a young adult, he now has a tender heart for living with integrity among his friends.

How about the values of fairness or courage? How many of our kids learned to play fair with their siblings the first time? How many of our kids were deathly afraid of something but instantly overcame it and showed courage? Not many, right? Developing values and life-giving habits takes training, working through successes and failures, and doing these things over time.

So here's my question. Why is it that we are okay with patiently guiding and training our children to help them learn the essential values of honesty, fairness, and courage, but we expect our kids to learn the virtue of chastity the first time, flawlessly, without ever messing up? If we idolize this expectation, then when they falter, they feel labeled, shamed, and judged by us and others.

I am certainly not condoning sexual permissiveness any more than I would excuse dishonesty or cowardice. Rather, I'm advocating that we simply be consistent with our parental expectations and realize that chastity, like any other virtue, is one that our kids will have to grow into. A helpful book in this regard is *Real Sex: The Naked*

*Truth About Chastity* by Lauren Winner. She became a believer in her early twenties after she had been sexually active. She says she had to learn how to be chaste. It wasn't in her nature; she had not practiced it. And she didn't do it just like that, but the Holy Spirit at work in her life helped her learn to become chaste.[5] Coming to understand chastity as a virtue that must be learned will also keep us from feeling like we're the worst parents in the world when our children stumble sexually. To the contrary, we can now view their struggles and failures as opportunities to take steps toward spiritual growth and maturity.

### Be the leading and most loving voice on sex in your children's lives.

I began this chapter by sharing with you our false start with having "the talk." As I reflect on that fateful night, I want to draw two conclusions. First, though the outcome was not what Robin had hoped for, I must give her credit for pursuing the value that we parents need to be the leading and most loving voice in our children's lives when it comes to this issue. Second, by referring to it as "the talk," we reveal every parent's wishful but misguided thinking that a single talk is all it takes. One and done. The truth, though, is that to inculcate the value of chastity, we must have many conversations along the path of our kids' growth journeys.

Before they hear it from anyone else, your children need to hear you regularly holding up the truths that sex is God's good gift, that it blesses our lives when we enjoy it the right way, and that when we misuse it, we will miss God's best in our relational lives. Without hesitation, cast a vision for God's desire for them in their future married lives. As a father of three boys, I can tell you, they are interested! At other times along the way, also hold out the reality of God's forgiveness and redeeming grace. Let them know that if they should ever falter in this area of their lives, God will continue to love them and work in their lives for his very best. These two truths are the essential seeds that must be planted for chastity and healthy intimacy to blossom into sexual wholeness.

One deal Robin struck with our boys was particularly helpful. She loves movies and quality TV shows, and the boys grew to share that love with her. As they got older, and as our culture's mores changed, it was hard for them to watch much that did not include inappropriate use of sex in the story line. So she made a covenant with them. Whenever they watched something that included a view of sex not in keeping with our values, they had a conversation with her about the scene when the show was over.

This gave her many organic occasions to talk about the character's sexual choices, the consequences, the effect on the people with whom they were involved, and the wisdom of God's way. All the while, she also assured them of God's forgiveness and redeeming grace and his desire to transform them in every area of their lives, including this one. This approach may not work for your family, but the bottom line is to simply stay engaged with your children in these conversations!

## Train your children to delay gratification.

To remain chaste obviously requires a willingness to delay gratification—a habit that is getting harder and harder to develop in today's world. Make no mistake, it is a habit that can be learned, and doing so can have a positive impact on practically every area of your children's lives. I have a friend named Corey who is a very intentional parent, and one day he shared with me that he was training his son Carter to delay gratification.

As they began a meal, he told Carter that if he chose to eat his dessert immediately after his meal, he would get one cookie. But if he waited an hour, he would receive three cookies. Simple but effective.

Not long after he began the training, they took a trip to Six Flags. As they got to their favorite roller coaster, there was a longer line for a seat in the front car. Carter surveyed the situation and said, "Hey,

Dad, I want to ride in the front car. It's going to take longer to wait in line, but it'll be more fun." He's learning the lesson of delayed gratification. You can teach your children this life skill if you are intentional. Create situations, like Corey did, where your children can exercise their gratification muscles. If you do this consistently, the habits they develop will serve them well as they think through the decisions they will face when it comes to having sex.

### Demonstrate a life of full devotion to Christ (which includes chastity).

This practice may be the single most influential factor in your child developing the virtue of chastity. The way you demonstrate a life of full devotion to God, which includes your own chastity, leaves an indelible mark on your child's heart and perception. You know you can't get your kids to keep their rooms clean if you've had underwear lying on your bedroom floor for more than a week. They can tell by your actions that it's not that important to you. Make no mistake, if your kids get on the computer and find a pornographic site in your browser history, you have just suffered a huge loss in your credibility to teach your kids chastity. If you're a single parent and have romantic partners spending the night at your house, your kids are getting a message—and it's likely not the message you want to give them.

Until you become chaste in your own spirit and actions, you have little hope of developing chastity in your child. On the other hand, when your kids see you living out this value, and you are having conversations with them about the whys behind your choices, you will maximize your efforts to help them succeed.

### Cast a vision for God's greater purposes in your children's lives.

One afternoon I was speaking to our student pastor, and he shared with me a trend he was noticing. "Jim, you wouldn't believe what's happening. We've got kids actively involved with sex, drugs, and alcohol. But when these kids realize that God has a greater purpose for their lives, they perk up. When I tell them, 'God wants you to be an influence on middle schoolers and other kids in your class, but you can't be an influence if you're involved in these things,' they're beginning to think, 'Wow, God may really want to do something in me and through me!'" As a result, he continued, "They're beginning to sense a larger and grander purpose. Many kids today have everything. Out of boredom they turn to sex, drugs, and alcohol. When the best things our culture can offer doesn't fulfill them, they get increasingly demotivated." Hearing of a grander vision and purpose for their lives truly becomes a greater affection and changes their perspective on sexual involvement.

I was greatly encouraged to hear how the approach one of our small group Bible studies for sixth-grade girls was modeling this very thing. They had been going through *Kisses from Katie*, a book about 19-year-old Katie Davis from Brentwood, Tennessee, who moved to Uganda to begin caring for children who were dying from malnutrition and other results of profound poverty. Katie created a ministry called Amazima that has transformed the lives of hundreds of children and families. The leader of this group of sixth-grade girls, Suzette, cast a vision that they, with God's help, could follow Katie's example and change a part of their world. I thought you might be encouraged by the email she sent her girls.

> I, truly, with all my heart, believe that God has a purpose for each of you. Like Katie in the book, you can know that purpose at a very young age. You don't have to wait to graduate from high school or college to really get to work. Your work is right here, right now. If you're not sure where to start, Jesus had a pretty great idea on where to begin. These are his words just days before he would go to the cross for you and for me:
>
>> For I was hungry and you gave me something to eat,
>> I was thirsty and you gave me something to drink,

I was a stranger and you invited me in, I needed clothes and you clothed me, I was sick and you looked after me, I was in prison and you came to visit me…Truly I tell you, whatever you did for one of the least of these brothers and sisters of mine, you did for me (Matthew 25:35-36,40).

I gave each of you jars to set on your kitchen table. They contained what for many in our world is their whole day's allotment of food. This verse from Matthew is on it for a reason. When you are tempted to get down or focus on yourself, don't forget God and all He has done…take a look at the jar and count your blessings. Then go and share those blessings with someone who needs a touch from Jesus! I cannot tell you how proud I am of you! Sixth-grade girls can change the world one person at a time. It all starts with you…today…go and be a blessing!…Love you!…Miss Suzette

When we as parents cast this kind of vision for a grander purpose for the lives of our children, we introduce what one writer calls "the expulsive power of a new affection."[6] He is pointing out that the best way to conquer sin is by surpassing it with a greater affection. Jesus hinted at this strongly in the beatitudes, where he teaches us, "Blessed are the pure in heart, for they shall see God" (Matthew 5:8). When we live out a life of purity, we will get to see God at work in and through our lives in a way that we would not otherwise. You can hardly give your child a better and more lasting gift than this!

........................................................

*Dear Lord,*

*Help. Help. Help. We live in such a sex-saturated world. The lie that sex can be separated from intimacy without effects pervades our culture. The beauty, purity, and sacredness of your blessed gift has been*

*lost. Please help me and my children see sex for the good gift it is. And help us use it correctly, in the ways you intend, so that our lives may be full and free to honor you. Protect my children as much as you can while I protect them as much as I can from the perceptions and images of sex that will harm them. And give me the grace and wisdom to model and teach the perceptions and attitudes toward sex that will give them a compelling vision of your gracious gift of intimacy.*

*Amen.*

## Breaking It Down for Every Age

Talking about sex in an instructive and healthy manner is a daunting prospect for most parents, no matter how young or old their kids may be. Here are a few guidelines to keep in mind as you're having these important discussions with your elementary-aged kids, tweens, and teens.

### Elementary-Aged Kids

When your child enters school and her circle of influence widens, remember that she is more likely to come to you with questions about sex if you have already established yourself as the leading and most loving voice on that topic. One way to signal your trustworthiness as the leading and most loving voice is by simply acknowledging the sexually charged content that your child encounters every day. Whether it's an inappropriate magazine cover in a checkout line or a scene in a TV show we couldn't turn off quite fast enough, our first instinct as parents is often to gloss over or ignore these uncomfortable encounters. Choose instead to calmly lean in to these moments as opportunities for chastity training. Reinforce to your child that sex is God's good gift and that it is enjoyed most fully in the context of marriage. Explain that even though we might see such images on TV or at the store, God asks that we treat sex as something special and private between a married couple.

## Tweens

The tween years offer the perfect training ground for chastity by developing the discipline of delayed gratification. During this season of life, for example, your preteen is likely becoming more firmly entrenched in a digital world that offers instant connection and the immediate gratification of virtual "likes." Help your tween disentangle himself from the lure of immediate gratification by setting intentional boundaries around screen time and social media. Setting these intentional boundaries—and talking with your tween about their importance—can go a long way toward helping him develop the discipline of delayed gratification. During the tween years, your child will experience increased exposure to sexually explicit content on the internet. Chapter 8 of this book deals with the tough topic of pornography and how to address this challenge at every stage of your child's life.

## Teens

News headlines and entertainment media will provide ample opportunity to initiate conversations with your teen about the consequences of sexual behavior if you simply make yourself available to talk. Your teen will be constantly inundated by messages about sex that fall short of God's intended purpose. Counter those messages by consistently casting a vision of God's design for sex and of God's greater purposes in her life. Try not to react with judgment, shame, or panic when your teen comes to you with such questions. Become your teen's biggest cheerleader, especially when you see her displaying self-discipline or self-leadership in ways that are big or small. And remember that as your teen grows in the virtue of chastity, she won't practice it perfectly. Keep the lines of communication open as you consistently hold up the vision for God's good gift of sex.

## Questions for Personal Reflection or Group Discussion

1. Have you had "the talk" with your kids? If so, how did it go? If not, why not?

2. How does the Bible's view of sex relate to your personal story? Do you believe, deep down, that sex is a good gift from God? How have you been blessed when you have been faithful to God's design for sex? What blessings have you missed when you have crossed God's boundary lines for sex?

3. As you reflect now, what do you truly want for your children's intimate lives when they become adults?

4. What are some ways you can become and remain your children's most influential voice on sex?

5. How can you model chastity in your own life and give your children a positive example by which to lead their own lives?

## Additional Resources

If you are interested in further reading on this subject, these resources may be helpful.

### For Parents

*Inside of Me* by Shellie R. Warren

*Real Sex: The Naked Truth About Chastity* by Lauren Winner

*Sex for Christians* by Lewis Smedes

## For Children and Teens

*God's Design for Sex* (series of four books) by Brenna Jones

*The Bare Facts: 39 Questions Your Parents Hope You Never Ask About Sex* by Josh McDowell

*The Purity Code: God's Plan for Sex and Your Body* by Jim Burns

*The Talk: 7 Lessons to Introduce Your Child to Biblical Sexuality* by Luke Gilkerson

# 5

# Other Religions

## Paul Basden

It's Friday afternoon at three, and you're sitting in the carpool line waiting to pick up your daughter from school. You don't want to stare, but you can't help noticing how different some of the kids look as they file out of the building. They don't look anything like your classmates did back in the day. A boy is wearing a white skull cap with a black Star of David on top. A girl is wearing a colorful Indian sari. A handful of students are talking to each other in a language that's not English. When your daughter comes out and says good-bye to them, they all smile and return her good-bye in perfect English but with a slight accent you can't identify.

If it hasn't been obvious to you before, it is now—your child is growing up in a world of different races, ethnicities, and yes, religions. It may have happened subtly and without fanfare, but religion in America has changed.

- Religion used to make people yawn. Now it makes them fight.
- Religion use to be boring and predictable. Now it's exciting, sometimes terrifyingly so.

- Religion used to be static. Now it's so dynamic you can't keep up with the changes.

Think back just a few generations. In 1955, the dominant religious landscape in America could be described as "Protestant, Catholic, Jew."[1] Not so today. A 2015 poll that asked 35,000 Americans to identify their religious preferences reveals that the landscape of faith is indeed changing. Fewer and fewer people self-identify as Christians while more and more claim no religious affiliation, usually preferring to be called atheist, agnostic, or "nones." As Christians are shrinking as a percentage of the population, other faiths are growing rapidly. Among non-Christian world religions, Muslims and Hindus have experienced the greatest growth in the United States.[2]

If you are tempted to ignore this development as unimportant to your family, I hope you will reconsider. This revolution in religion is relevant to you and your children for several reasons. First, if you are a Christian, many in our culture will label you as exclusive and intolerant. Christianity claims that Jesus is Savior and Lord of the world. Countless people regard that as a bigoted and elitist statement. Yet it's at the heart of your faith, and to alter it would be to alter the Christian message. Jesus said, "I am the way and the truth and the life. No one comes to the Father except through me" (John 14:6). Today such a belief is seen as narrow-minded. Your children will likely hear that charge when they talk to their friends about their faith.

Second, your world is shrinking. Unique and exotic world religions used to be "somewhere out there." Now they're right here, as near as the local mosque, temple, or synagogue—not to mention the classroom. And they are here to stay.

Third, everyone's long-term safety and security depend on a deeper understanding among people of different religions. World peace is more contingent than ever upon people of diverse faiths finding a way to live together without killing each other. Think about

Hindus and Christians in India, Muslims and Jews in Israel, and Catholics and Protestants in Northern Ireland. If religions were to engage in healthy conversation rather than in hateful confrontation, wouldn't peace be more prevalent?

If you are like me, this issue may have sneaked up on you. While you were going to church and trying to raise your kids to follow Jesus Christ, a whole new world grew up around you. And the presence of other religions is now the norm, not the exception. I want to help you get ready for some tough conversations. To be an effective parent, you will need a wise answer to this question: What do we tell our kids about other religions? But don't expect a simple answer.

Because the topic is both complex and global, I will offer two sets of answers—basic and advanced. Since you know your child best, you can match your answers to their age or curiosity. Let's start with the basics.

## Religion Is Everywhere

According to students of culture, all people everywhere are religious. If you define religion as how people try to relate to a god or supreme being, then it's no stretch to say that religion is a universal phenomenon. To my knowledge, there has never been a culture devoid of spiritual beliefs and practices. Evangelist Billy Graham, who preached the gospel around the world, said he found religion everywhere. I once heard him say, "Wherever I go, I see people bowing down beside the great rivers of the world. And whether they are kneeling on the banks of the Nile, Ganges, Amazon, or Mississippi, they are kneeling to pray to their God or gods. Everyone is religious!"

Not everyone may attend a worship service or read a holy book or pray to a god—but everyone is religious. All people order their lives around someone or something they consider all-important. It may be Allah or Buddha or Krishna. It may be Moses or Jesus or Joseph Smith. Some people may say they are atheistic and irreligious, yet their atheism serves as their religion, for they bow before it, believe it, and treat it as absolute. Religion seems to be part of what it means to be human. Help your children realize that everyone is religious.

## Look for the Good

All religions have something good and true in them. This statement, properly understood, is the basic building block for helping your child respect others with different religious beliefs. C.S. Lewis was unapologetic on this point when he wrote, "If you are a Christian, you do not have to believe that all the other religions are simply wrong all through...you are free to think that all these religions, even the queerest ones, contain at least some hint of the truth."[3]

Some Christians are not comfortable with this conviction, believing instead that all non-Christian religions are completely false. Their reasoning goes like this:

> If Jesus is the Son of God and the only way to God,
> and if other religions don't believe this about Jesus,
> then every religion but Christianity must be false.

I understand this logic, and it points to a basic Christian belief regarding salvation: Jesus is the only way to God. But it overstates the case regarding the possibility of truth in other religions. It fails to take into consideration New Testament passages such as Paul's encounter with idolaters in Athens. Notice how the apostle to the Gentiles finds truth in the other religions of his day.

> While Paul was waiting for them in Athens, he was deeply troubled by all the idols he saw everywhere in the city...He went to the synagogue to reason with the Jews and the God-fearing Gentiles, and he spoke daily in the public square to all who happened to be there.
>
> He also had a debate with some of the Epicurean and Stoic philosophers...Then they took him to the high council of the city...Paul, standing before the council, addressed

them as follows: "Men of Athens, I notice that you are very religious in every way, for as I was walking along I saw your many shrines. And one of your altars had this inscription on it: 'To an Unknown God.' This God, whom you worship without knowing, is the one I'm telling you about.

"He is the God who made the world and everything in it. Since he is Lord of heaven and earth, he doesn't live in man-made temples, and human hands can't serve his needs—for he has no needs. He himself gives life and breath to everything, and he satisfies every need. From one man he created all the nations throughout the whole earth. He decided beforehand when they should rise and fall, and he determined their boundaries.

"His purpose was for the nations to seek after God and perhaps feel their way toward him and find him—though he is not far from any one of us. For in him we live and move and exist. As some of your own poets have said, 'We are his offspring.' And since this is true, we shouldn't think of God as an idol designed by craftsmen from gold or silver or stone" (Acts 17:16-19,22-29 NLT).

Who would have guessed that Paul would appeal to the fragments of truth found in a Cretan philosopher (Epimenides) and a Stoic philosopher (Aratus) to teach about the Christian God? But he did. Why? Because he knew that all religions have something good and true in them even though they are incomplete. They have some light in them, but they need the One True Light, Jesus Christ, to brighten their way and lead them to the One True God. This is the meaning of the prologue to John's Gospel: "The true light that gives light to everyone was coming into the world" (John 1:9).

To make this more concrete for your child, give them examples of how different religions have elements of truth in them. For example...

*Judaism is known for a heightened sense of moral justice, seen especially in the message of the Old Testament prophets.* Sally Becker went to Bosnia in 1993 to put justice into practice by giving aid to innocent child victims of war. While serving there, she was jailed by Serbian soldiers and shot in the face by masked gunmen. She not only survived but also continued her work. Her heroic efforts helped save hundreds of lives through evacuation and medical aid during her stay in the war-torn Balkans. Her Jewish faith guided her quest to ensure that right would defeat wrong.[4]

*Islam requires good deeds of its followers, as enumerated in the Five Pillars.* I have a Muslim friend who lives in Africa. He is one of the most grace-filled men I know. I would entrust my life to him—in fact, I do just that whenever I travel to his country on a mission trip, because he is our driver. Despite the negative press Muslims have received because of radical terrorists, this Muslim lives out the faith of Abraham in wonderful ways.

*Mormonism excels at emphasizing family values.* Many years ago, a Mormon family in California befriended a little girl who lived in their neighborhood. The family, composed of twelve children, welcomed this only child into their loving home, took her to church with them on Sundays, and gave her the first Bible she ever owned. Here is how she tells the story:

> I used to beg to spend the night and weekends at their home. I had a lot of fun growing up with that family: camping, going to piano lessons and recitals, singing in church, praying as a family, visiting the Temple at Christmas, and just having plain old fun with all the kids. I appreciate the way they loved and cared for me and wonder what would have happened to me if they had not been a part of my life. I believe it was all a part of God's protection and plan to lead me to where I am today.

Living out the truth as they knew it, this Mormon family became a surrogate family to a little girl who was spiritually hungry. Today that little girl is a wife and mother, a faithful Christ-follower, and a dynamic church leader.

If you know, admire, and respect anyone who adheres to a non-Christian faith, speak positively to your child about that person. Explain that their religion, while incomplete in your eyes, has an element of truth in it. Teach your children not to be afraid of people who subscribe to a religion other than Christianity. Help your kids look for the good in people of all faiths. Find ways to connect with them as friends, even if they have yet to name Jesus as Lord. Above all, model for your children how to be respectful and kind, not fearful or hateful, to those who follow other beliefs. If you are a Christ-follower, you know that hate comes from fear, and love comes from God, for "perfect love drives out fear" (1 John 4:18).

Help your child see that all religions have something good and true in them.

## Note the Differences

Show your kids that all religions are not the same. Begin by explaining that different religions worship different kinds of gods.

- Hinduism believes in many gods (polytheism), while Judaism, Christianity, and Islam all believe in just one God (monotheism).

- Buddhism, Taoism, and Hinduism believe in impersonal gods (pantheism or deism), whereas the monotheistic religions believe in a personal God (theism).

- Some religions claim that God spoke through a human. Islam teaches that Allah spoke through Mohammed, and Judaism affirms that Yahweh spoke through Moses. But Christianity claims that God revealed himself through a God-man, Jesus, who is the exact image of God.

At school, your child may be learning about various religions and what they teach. As you review their studies with them, point out that each faith is different from the others on several major matters. Here is a simple chart of the four major world religions that you can use as a summary with your kids:[5]

| | Judaism | Islam | Hinduism | Christianity |
|---|---|---|---|---|
| **Name of God** | Yahweh, who is holy | Allah, who is all-powerful | Brahman, who is absolute and impersonal | God, who is Father, Son, and Spirit |
| **Key person(s)** | Abraham, Moses, David | Muhammad | Many swamis, or teachers | Jesus |
| **Authority** | Jewish Scripture | Koran | Vedas | Bible, especially the New Testament |
| **Salvation** | keeping covenant | obeying the Five Pillars | reincarnation and reuniting with Brahman | reconciliation with God by grace through faith |
| **Jesus** | teacher and prophet | teacher and prophet | one of millions of gods | eternal Son of God who became human |

You can safely tell your child that all religions are not the same—and never claim to be.

## It's All About Jesus

Jesus is what makes Christianity different from all other religions. This is the heart of the matter and where you need to highlight two very important points.

First, tell your kids that as Christians, we believe our religion is true. C.S. Lewis offered a counterpoint to his earlier statement about other religions having an element of truth in them:

> But of course, Christianity does mean thinking that where Christianity differs from other religions, Christianity is right and they are wrong. As in arithmetic, there is only one right answer to a sum, and all other answers are wrong; but some of the wrong answers are much nearer being right than others.[6]

This view is called an exclusive claim to truth. "Exclusivism" sounds elitist and judgmental to some. But it doesn't mean Christians think they are better than those who follow other religions—as though the church were a club for sinless saints rather than a hospital for flawed sinners. It means Christians think Jesus made absolute claims about himself, about God, and about salvation, which we believe are true. This belief rejects the notion that other religions also are the way to God.

Those who are not Christians may be deeply bothered by this exclusivist claim, but they shouldn't be. All religions are exclusive. All religions believe they are right. Nobody follows a religion because they think it is wrong. Even people who believe there is no God believe they are right—in other words, atheists are exclusive in their absolute claim that God does not exist!

Teach your children that the essence of Christianity is the belief that Jesus is the unique Son of God and the only way to God. Help them articulate it in their own words as you help them believe it is true.

The second important thing you want to tell your kids is that Jesus separates Christianity from all other religions. When you compare the figure of Jesus with the founder of all other religions, you find a world of difference. For example, Christians believe that...

- *Jesus is the incarnation of God.* Jesus of Nazareth is the eternal Son of God who was born in Bethlehem to the Virgin Mary and lived his life wholly devoted to God and free from sin. When he died, his death was the sacrifice of a perfect life to a perfect God for imperfect people like you and me. God raised him back to life on the third day to show that Jesus was who he said he was.
- *Jesus is the revelation of God.* Everything Jesus said 2,000 years ago was true then and is still true today. When he spoke, God was speaking through him. When he acted, God was acting through him. Jesus revealed God clearly.
- *Jesus is the grace of God.* Jesus came to earth as a gift from God to all people everywhere. The gift is new life that brings with it a new relationship to God, to others, to creation, and to ourselves. As you may have heard before, this is ultimately the difference between "do" and "done." Other religions stress what you must *do* to appease or please their deity, but Christianity asserts that Jesus has *done* all that is necessary to reconcile us to God. That is grace.

Embrace the opportunity to tell your children about what God's grace means to you and how it has changed your life. As you tell them who Jesus is in the Bible, you can show and tell them who Jesus is to you.

Simply said, what sets Christianity apart from all other religions is the belief that in Jesus, God got his hands dirty. Other religions are about intellectual ideas such as reincarnation, karma, and Nirvana. But Christianity is about a person. Clarify for your kids that Christianity as a religion doesn't save—only Jesus saves!

## The Universal Language

All people of all religions understand only one language—love. Keeping in mind the order of "show and tell," remind your kids that their first task is to show love. By their actions, they can show that God loves all people, regardless of religion. By smiling first, using courteous language, and offering respect, kids can win over those who are suspicious of Christianity.

Along with showing, telling is also important. Encourage your children to tell their friends that God loves everyone. Encourage them to enjoy friendships with kids of other faiths. Encourage them to get comfortable saying what Jesus means in their own lives. Remember that the power of the gospel is real even (or especially) when it comes from the lips of little children.

Bottom line: Lead your child to resist all resentment toward those who belong to other religions. That is not the way of love, and therefore, it is not the way of Jesus. As one author has wisely warned, "We do not glorify Jesus Christ by slandering adherents of other religions."[7]

These are the five most important things you can tell your children about other religions. While you will customize these answers, they contain the basic information for children of all ages.

As your kids get older, however, get ready to discuss some deeper topics with them. Here are some advanced answers on this subject.

## Three Important "Isms"

There are three "isms" your child will hear or read about in discussions about religions. You should be familiar with them if you want to have meaningful conversations with your kids.

### Pluralism

This is the belief that all religions are equally true. This is not simply saying that many religions claim to be true. Pluralism asserts that all religions, no matter how different their beliefs may be, are equally valid avenues to God. The problem with this ism is that if all religions claim to be correct, yet all religions have different beliefs, then how can all religions be true? Pluralists answer that you can believe anything you want—and as long as it's your own private belief, then it can be true for you. They argue that this approach to truth is not valid in science or mathematics or any other field of knowledge dealing with facts but is valid in religion because beliefs are merely private opinions. They conclude that all religions can be equally true since beliefs are simply sentiments without any claim to facts.

In reply, Christians believe that Jesus's life is a matter of public historical record and therefore should be treated as a fact, not as an opinion. Other religions are built on ideas, but Christianity stands or falls on a historical truth claim: Jesus of Nazareth lived, was crucified, and was raised back to life. Bono, the Irish music icon, argued the Christian viewpoint well: "[Jesus] went around saying he was the Messiah. That's why he was crucified. He was crucified because he said he was the Son of God. So, he either, in my view, was the Son of God or he was nuts. Forget rock-and-roll messianic complexes, I mean Charlie Manson–type delirium."[8] Christians believe Jesus was neither nuts nor delirious. We believe he told the truth about who he was and who God is. And we believe that his life, death, and resurrection stand the test of historical scrutiny. All of this points to the fact that Christians do not believe in pluralism as defined above.

## Relativism

This is the popular belief that says, "My truth is just as valid as your truth, so there can be no absolute truth." Some relativists go so far as to say that nobody can even find truth because it is unknowable. Regardless, all truth is relative. But this makes no logical sense. The claim that all truth is relative is itself an absolute claim. It says, "Here is an absolute truth you can build your life on: There is no absolute truth." We should not be embarrassed to reject such faulty reasoning and to recognize a smoke-and-mirrors trick when we hear it. We are wise to regard the claim of relativism as meaningless.

## Universalism

This is the belief that all people will eventually be saved and that God must and will do this to earn our devotion. As Christians, we can see several problems with this claim. First, Jesus clearly refers to a sin that can never be forgiven: "Whoever blasphemes against the Holy Spirit will never be forgiven; they are guilty of an eternal sin" (Mark 3:29).[9] At the very least, this statement means that not everyone will be saved. Second, to accept universalism is to accept the idea that God forces people, even against their will, to be saved. Such a view of God flies in the face of a robust belief in human freedom. Third, universalism belittles God's great gift in Jesus Christ. Were Jesus's incarnation, crucifixion, and resurrection all for naught? Did God send his Son into the world to save us, knowing full well that our response would have no impact on our eternity because he has already determined eventually to save everyone? Orthodox Christianity has never affirmed universalism as defined above.

These three isms can be intimidating, but they are not impossible to understand. Older children, especially teens, can comprehend them. They need you as a parent to be a thoughtful discussion partner who will listen to their questions and help them find the truth.

## Three Harder Questions

One would think that the question of what to tell our kids about other religions is tough enough to answer. But as it turns out, some related questions are even tougher. They are likely to be asked by teens, but don't underestimate the curiosity of young children when it comes to spiritual concerns. Here are three challenging questions your kids may pose at some point. I hope these answers will prepare you for those conversations.

### Should Christians believe in religious liberty for people of all faiths?

A conversation about other religions may not lead into a discussion about politics, but I hope you will take the plunge if the opportunity arises. The bloodiest conflicts in our world are often fueled by religious rhetoric, so you will do your children a favor if you can clarify the relationship between religion and government. For Christians, the belief in an exclusive truth does not mean that we push our way into the halls of power to use politics to favor the adherents of our religion and punish those of other religions.

When church and state have merged, the results have usually been ugly for everyone. If your child is up for a couple of examples from Western history, you can remind them of these:

- In eleventh- and twelfth-century Europe, the Holy Roman Empire (government) and the Holy Catholic Church (religion) conspired to send armies to Jerusalem to kill Muslims so they could reclaim Jerusalem as a Christian city. Although done in Jesus's name, nothing about the Crusades was Christian.

- In fifteenth-century Spain, King Ferdinand and Queen Isabella (government) ordered the Holy Catholic Church (religion) to conduct an inquisition against all Jews and Turks (Muslims) to "give them a chance" to become Christians. Those who said no were exiled, tortured, or killed. Although justified as a form of evangelism, there was no good news in the Inquisition.

Teach your children that Christians believe in religious liberty for all people. We do not believe we should co-opt government to force people to adopt the Christian faith or any other faith against their will. We believe that Christianity is true, but we don't use our religion as a hammer to harm those of other faiths.

### Does God love those who follow other religions?

Start with the good news: God loves all people in the world and wants them to have eternal life. Highlight these great New Testament passages:

- "For God so loved the world that he gave his one and only Son, that whoever believes in him shall not perish but have eternal life. For God did not send his Son into the world to condemn the world, but to save the world through him" (John 3:16-17).

- "God was reconciling the world to himself in Christ, not counting people's sins against them" (2 Corinthians 5:19).
- "God our Savior…wants all people to be saved and to come to a knowledge of the truth. For there is one God and one mediator between God and mankind, the man Christ Jesus, who gave himself as a ransom for all people" (1 Timothy 2:3-6).
- "The Lord…is patient with you, not wanting anyone to perish, but everyone to come to repentance" (2 Peter 3:9).
- "We have seen and testify that the Father has sent his Son to be the Savior of the world" (1 John 4:14).

Explain to your kids that God's disposition toward anyone who adheres to any religion (or to no religion) is love. That should be automatic in our thinking, for God is love (1 John 4:8,16 NLT). God's love doesn't automatically save anyone or everyone, especially against their will. But his disposition is a love that draws people and saves all who turn to him.

At this point your kids may ask, "What about all those people who lived prior to Jesus, who never had a chance to be saved?" Great question!

Tell them that before Christ came into the world, God still loved all people and saved them when they placed their faith in his mercy. To illustrate this truth, invite your child to open the Bible to Hebrews 11 and read the stirring stories of Old Testament heroes who lived by faith. As you recount their lives of obedience and trust, ask your child, "Where do you think those people are now?" Hopefully they will say, "Heaven!" Then confirm their answer by reading the first verse of Hebrews 12, which refers to these men and women who lived prior to Jesus's birth: "Therefore, since we are surrounded by such a great cloud of witnesses…" Those Old Testament heroes are in heaven with God, cheering on all of us here on earth! Tell your child that before Jesus came into the world, God saved people who believed his promise and trusted in his grace.

If your child is especially precocious, he or she may push the envelope even further by asking, "What about all those people who have been born since Christ came to earth but who never had a chance to hear the good news or respond to it? How does God treat them?" This is one of the toughest questions around. Here's how I tackle it.

Begin by reminding your child that God is compassionate to all, not just to those who are nice. In fact, God is as gracious to unkind people as he is to kind people. We have it on the authority of Jesus: "Your Father in heaven...causes his sun to rise on the evil and the good, and sends rain on the righteous and the unrighteous" (Matthew 5:45).

Then explain that God delights in blessing people everywhere, leaving clues about himself in the process, hoping that those who receive his bountiful blessings will trace the gifts back to the Giver. As Paul clarified to a group of idolaters in Lystra, "[God] has not left himself without testimony: He has shown kindness by giving you rain from heaven and crops in their seasons; he provides you with plenty of food and fills your hearts with joy" (Acts 14:17).

At this point you are establishing the baseline that God loves the world and is indiscriminately kind to everyone. That certainly includes people devoted to other religions.

Now we come to the question of the destiny of those who have never been evangelized.

### If people who belong to other religions never hear of Christ, can they ever be saved?

Remember, you are not referring to individuals who have heard and rejected the gospel, but those who have never heard and therefore never had a chance to respond. Here are three ways Christians have answered this challenging question.

First is the majority answer for the past two millennia: exclusivism. It teaches that Jesus is the only way to God. Salvation is available only to those who hear and accept the gospel. Those who never receive the good news are eternally lost.

Second is an answer we've already discussed above: pluralism. It argues that all religions are true and legitimate ways to God; therefore, all people are saved. As mentioned above, this view entails the flawed belief that God must and will save all people.

Third is a minority answer that has gained some popularity in the past few decades: inclusivism. It affirms that while Jesus is the only way to God, God's grace is available to those who never hear the name of Jesus or the gospel—so long as they fall on God's mercy in faith, regardless of the religious language they employ.

I wish I could resolve this last question for you fully, but I can't. The mystery is simply too big, and my brain is too small. However, these are the moments when I find great comfort in two Scripture passages that remind me that God knows and can be trusted with what I can never know—including this question about the destiny of the unevangelized.

The first passage is found near the end of Deuteronomy. Moses is reminding the Israelites who are awaiting entry into the Promised Land that God has made a gracious covenant with them, but they must keep their part of the covenant or God will judge them. As if to save them from speculating about what might happen in an unknown future, Moses reiterates that they are responsible only for what they can control—their own obedience.

> The Lord our God has secrets known to no one. We are not accountable for them, but we and our children are accountable forever for all that he has revealed to us, so that we may obey all the terms of these instructions (Deuteronomy 29:29 NLT).

The second passage occurs centuries later. The apostle Paul, himself an Israelite, is agonizing over the reality that fewer and fewer Jews are following Jesus as Messiah. After writing at length to the church at Rome on the destiny of disobedient Israelites, he concludes Romans 9–11 with a humble admission of his own intellectual limitations and a joyful burst of gratitude to God, who knows all and is utterly trustworthy.

> Oh, the depth of the riches of the wisdom and knowl-
> edge of God!
> How unsearchable his judgments,
> and his paths beyond tracing out!
> "Who has known the mind of the Lord?
> Or who has been his counselor?"
> "Who has ever given to God,
> that God should repay them?"
> For from him and through him and for him are all things.
> To him be the glory forever! Amen (Romans 11:33-36).

The answer to this last question remains a mystery. But in the end, we can trust God to be as merciful as he is just and as just as he is merciful. And we can pray harder than ever as we seek to share the gospel with people in every culture, remembering these challenging words:

> So we tell others about Christ, warning everyone and teach-
> ing everyone with all the wisdom God has given us. We
> want to present them to God, perfect in their relationship
> to Christ. That's why I work and struggle so hard, depend-
> ing on Christ's mighty power that works within me (Colos-
> sians 1:28-29 NLT).

## Conclusion

Few questions are more common or controversial than that of other religions. In our increasingly pluralistic culture, your children may know more Muslims and Hindus, and more about them, than you do. The answer is not to go hide your head in the sand. The answer is to learn more about other religions, dig deeper into your own Christian faith, and be glad that Jesus makes all the difference.

*Dear God,*

*I believe that Jesus is God's best gift ever. I am seeking to build my life on Christ, and I want my children to do the same. I also want their friends who claim other religions to find the joy and peace of knowing Christ. Help me to model your love for all people so that my kids see it. Then help me lead my children to show and tell your love to all their friends so that they will want to receive your best gift ever— Jesus Christ.*

*Amen.*

## Breaking It Down for Every Age

The way you engage your kids in conversations about other religions will be different at every phase. Here are a few things to keep in mind as you talk with your younger kids, tweens, and teens.

### Elementary-Aged Kids

One of the realities of this developmental stage is that your kids are likely gaining their first exposure to many influences and cultures beyond your own. At school, with neighborhood friends, on sports teams, or in other extracurricular activities, your child's world is expanding. As parents, our first instinct is often to steer our kids toward people with backgrounds and cultures that closely resemble our own. While appropriate oversight is necessary at this stage, don't miss opportunities to help your kids forge friendships with those who might look, speak, or worship differently.

Simple, intentional demonstrations of kindness and friendship help set a real-life context of love for every conversation with your kids about people of other religions. When your kids ask questions about people from other cultures and religions, you can explain that while we might not agree with everything they believe, we should always show them love and respect, just as Jesus did.

## Tweens

As your kids move into the middle school years, their exposure to other religions will only increase. Stay attuned to what they're learning in school, as they will likely study world religions at some point during this phase. Your tween may not be as likely to initiate questions and conversations with you as he was in elementary school, but his schoolwork can be a wonderful springboard for some of the more advanced conversations outlined in this chapter. Find times in his schedule when he is most open to conversation (you may find this happens late at night, when you might be *least* inclined to discussion). Ask open-ended questions, and genuinely listen to what your kid is learning and processing about other religions. Supplement what he's learning in school with discussions about the uniqueness of Christianity among world religions, and highlight the things that set Jesus apart from all other religious leaders. Consider providing him with additional resources that can help him process his questions—such as *The Case for Faith for Kids*, listed below in the resources section.

## Teens

As high school students, your teens are likely considering the world (and their places in it) with an increased level of thoughtfulness. They are attuned to current events—perhaps even more than you realize—as their involvement in social media and exposure to the 24-hour news cycle increases. Rather than ignoring news stories that involve other religions, use current events as teachable moments to engage with your teen on this topic. As she gets older, your teen will likely begin to grapple with the more difficult questions addressed in this chapter, such as the fate of those who never hear the good news of Jesus. As you engage your kids in these more difficult conversations, remember that you don't have to have all the answers. It's okay—even helpful—for your kids to see you grappling with these questions in your own life, especially as you point them consistently toward the truth that we can trust God in all we don't understand because he has revealed himself to be trustworthy in Jesus.

## Questions for Personal Reflection or Group Discussion

1. Which non-Christian religions are your children most exposed to? What questions have they asked you about these religions?

2. Do you have any neighbors, coworkers, friends, or family members who adhere to a religion other than Christianity? If so, have you had any meaningful conversations about faith?

3. How would you answer this question: "How is Jesus different from the founders of the other major religions?" How would your child answer it?

4. How can your family express love in a practical way to a family of another faith?

## Additional Resources

If you are interested in further reading on this subject, these resources may be helpful.

### For Parents

*The Case for Faith* by Lee Strobel (chapter 5)

*The Complete Idiot's Guide to the World's Religions* by Brandon Toropov and Father Luke Buckles

*Faith Seeking Understanding* by Daniel Migliore (chapter 13)

*The Reason for God* by Tim Keller (chapter 1)

*So What's the Difference? A Look at 20 Worldviews, Faiths, and Religions and How They Compare to Christianity* by Fritz Ridenour

*The Supremacy of Jesus* by Stephen Neill

*A Wideness in God's Mercy: The Finality of Jesus Christ in a World of Religions* by Clark H. Pinnock

## For Children and Teens

*The Case for Faith for Kids (Updated and Expanded)* by Lee Strobel (chapter 4)

*The Case for Faith Student Edition* by Lee Strobel (chapter 4)

# 6

# Racism

## Jim Johnson

Our nation is struggling with violent seizures of racism, and few communities are left untouched. Just a couple of years ago, this was brought home to me in a very real way. On Tuesday morning, July 5, 2016, two white police officers shot and killed Alton Sterling, an African American man, outside a convenience store in Baton Rouge, Louisiana. The next day, Philando Castile, another African American man, was shot and killed by a police officer in a routine traffic stop in St. Paul, Minnesota. These two killings evoked mostly peaceful demonstrations in major cities across the United States—one of which occurred in Dallas, Texas, on Thursday evening. After an uneventful march, shots began to ring out. When the smoke and chaos cleared, five Dallas police officers lay dead. Seven other policemen and two civilians were also injured.

Micah Xavier Johnson, an African American Army veteran of two tours in Afghanistan, was cornered on the second floor of a nearby parking garage. According to Dallas police chief David Brown, himself an African American, Johnson confessed during several hours of intense negotiations that he was upset about the recent police shootings and that he wanted to kill white people, especially white officers.[1] When he refused to give up peacefully, Dallas police detonated a bomb placed by a robot near where Johnson was holed up. He did not survive.

Law enforcement officers, politicians, and community leaders struggle to ascertain how to help their constituencies sort through and make sense of the volatile dynamics that are running amok. But one thing is certain—these will not be the last eruptions of violence in our nation. As a result, you can count on your children asking, "What are all these protests and marches about?" "Why can't people from different races get along?" "Why do people exclude me just because of the color of my skin?" Your answers to these questions will have a significant impact on your children—and their children as well.

## Why Do We Still Struggle with Racism?

As you reflect on the latest instance of racial profiling or violence, you may be asking the same questions I'm asking: How can this still be happening? Haven't we made more progress than this? Aren't we living in the shadow of the reality of America's first black president?

The truth is, we have indeed made a lot of racial progress in recent years. Orlando Patterson, a Harvard sociologist, wrote at the turn of this century that the previous 50 years had been some of the most significant years in the history of mankind. He maintains that "the changes in racial attitudes, the guaranteeing of legal and political rights, and the expansion of economic opportunity are historically unparalleled."[2] However, we clearly have a lot of transforming work yet to do. And there are many hindrances and even forces that seem to be working against our best efforts. Before we begin to delve into practical ways to talk to kids about racism, I think it would be helpful to lay out the nature of some of the challenges we are facing so we can be better prepared to guide our children. Here are two reasons racism persists and continues to plague our land.

*All God's children have bias issues.*

Red and yellow, black and white, we all have biases in his sight. So do cops, preachers, bankers, masons, and fourth-grade teachers. You name them, and bias will claim them. The human default setting is to assume the best of our own kind and project the worst on others. Parental prejudices easily get passed down. Hurts and injustices of the past are bequeathed unresolved from one generation to the next. Pride and prejudice, anger and resentment, unforgiveness and violence are the encoded bytes of human nature. Whenever our hardware gets overheated by stress, loss, or fear, our operating system does an automatic reboot, and we return to the safety mode of our default settings. Bias for me and my kind carries the day again.

*We assume too much.*

The way we think, feel, and act is determined to a large degree by the assumptions we hold about the nature of reality. When those assumptions are properly aligned with the way things really are, they tend to serve us well. On the other hand, when there is a large gap between our presuppositions about life and reality itself, we set ourselves up for increased conflict and frustration. Here are three race-related assumptions that have not served us well.

*We assume a lot about a person simply based on their appearance.*

Whenever we see a person for the first time, our brain kicks into high gear, and we start filtering everything we see. We're thinking, "Are they safe, or are they not? Are they out to get me or here to help me? Do they want something from me, or can they offer something to me?" In a split second, based on the internal assumptions wired into our subconscious by what we have been taught and personally experienced, our brain starts assigning qualities, values, and characteristics to that person based solely on their appearance. In essence, we stereotype them and then we act accordingly.

Here's an example. When you saw my picture in this book, what did you notice? Gray hair, crow's feet, growing chrome dome on top. What conclusions did you quickly draw? Geezer. Irrelevant. Uncool. Probably can't remember where he puts his keys. But you would be wrong. My hair is not gray; it is platinum blond. I know that Kanye is married to Kim and their children's names are North, Saint, and Chicago. My five-year-old granddaughter thinks I am really hip, and she is younger and hipper than you, so there. And my keys are always in my front right pocket.

Now, my example is innocuous, and if you hold on to your presuppositions about guys with gray hair, crow's feet, and a balding pate, about the worst you can probably do to me is write a really rotten review on Amazon. But it's a different story if you are a seventh-grade Hispanic boy who goes to his local middle school, sees the cool white kids staring him down, and then hears them yell, "Hey, Juan"— which is not his real name—"why don't you go back to Mexico?" or "Hey, Juan, why don't you go mow my yard?" As long as we assume too much about other people based on the color of their skin or their ethnic background, there will always be events like those in St. Paul, Baton Rouge, and Dallas.

We assume our world is the same as other people's.

For the preponderance of people who are white, this is a land of equal opportunity. If you work hard, persevere, and are plucky enough, you can pull yourself up by your own bootstraps. What we don't see is that the deck has been stacked in our favor. Our country was founded by Anglo-Europeans for Anglo-Europeans, and the road to success slants in our direction.

If you are a minority, not only does the road not slant in your direction but there are walls and other obstacles that must be skirted, climbed, and sometimes pushed down. We all understand individual racism...one person thinking his or her race is superior and worthier than another. But white Americans like me often don't comprehend the idea of structural racism. Structural racism, simply put, occurs when a culture or society is structurally slanted to the advantage of one race and disadvantage of all others.

The trouble is, if you are white, you don't see the systemic and structural obstacles embedded in our culture. And most of us don't know anybody who does see or run into them. The *Washington Post* recently cited a study revealing that "for every 91 white friends a white American has, they have only one black friend." Additionally, "75 percent of whites have entirely white social networks without any minority presence."[3]

In order to gain more understanding, I met with George Yancey, an African American professor of sociology at the University of North Texas. I asked him to help me mentally grasp this reality, which is mostly invisible to me. Here's what he said.

> I grew up in Amarillo, Texas, and in high school, I had to get a job. In the black part of town, there was only a small grocery store, so there were practically no jobs to be had. As a result, I had to ride a bus to the other side of town to get a job. By the time I walked to the bus stop, waited for it to arrive, and then rode to my job it took one and a half hours one way. For me as a student, the economic structure of our community placed an additional three-hour burden on me if I wanted to get a job.

We can always point to exceptional individuals who are extremely talented, exert herculean effort, possess an uncanny power of perseverance, and rise to the top, but for the overwhelming majority of the minority, getting ahead is an uphill climb fraught with all kinds of walls and obstacles.

We assume that if we're not racist, we don't need to do anything about it.

Of the assumptions we too often make, this one might be the most insidious. I'm pretty sure it's impossible to live without some intrinsic biases. But given the multiculturalism emerging in our society, I do believe we can approach a perspective of different ethnicities that is no longer racist. There is a seductive nuance, however, to this way of thinking. We can easily tell ourselves that if we quash the impulses of bigotry in our own hearts, we have no further obligations.

Biblically, nothing could be further from the truth. Even a cursory reading of the Old Testament prophets reminds us that God has high expectations for his people when it comes to issues of social justice. Hear God speaking through Isaiah: "Learn to do good. Seek justice. Help the oppressed. Defend the cause of orphans. Fight for the rights of widows" (Isaiah 1:17 NLT). Note the action words—learn, do, seek, help, defend, fight for—God uses to spur us on to good actions and loving deeds on behalf of others. Thinking rightly about this issue is the beginning of a faithful response, but it is certainly not God's desired end. He's looking for actions too.

I'm embarrassed to say that this is the assumption that has inhibited my spiritual growth and leadership. Over the past 25 years, a blessed family experience has helped me deal with my own racial prejudice. My sister, Linda, was unable to have children of her own, so she and her husband, Chris, decided to adopt. First they adopted Natalie, a beautiful Caucasian girl. When they went to adopt a second child, they were asked if they would be open to adopting a biracial child. They prayed through the decision and said, "Yes, we're all in." Soon Abbey arrived, and her warm brown skin turned a lot of heads in the West Texas town where they lived. My sister and brother-in-law graciously put up with the well-meaning but incredulous question that has an obvious answer: "Yes, she's adopted."

Not long after Abbey was settled into her new family, another biracial child who needed a home came to Linda and Chris's attention. So they adopted Christian, the strong and swift son Chris had always desired. Still, their nest would not be full until Maddie, a precious and precocious African American girl, completed their brood. Watching Chris and Linda navigate the strong crosscurrents involved in parenting such a diverse little family under the gracious eye of God has been an inspiration and a living laboratory for me. As a result, most of my racial prejudices have slowly diminished through the years. However, I soon became self-satisfied with my personal development in this area and thought that my work was done…until Ferguson.

On August 9, 2014, Michael Brown, an 18-year-old African American male, was shot and killed by Ferguson, Missouri, police officer Darren Wilson. The resulting protests and rioting in Ferguson and other cities across America ignited anew the debate about racial injustice in our country. As a part of a series at our church in February 2015 titled "Trending," I was tasked with speaking God's truth and love into this roiling topic. As it turned out, I was at a conference in Florida the week before my message and ran into a pastor who had led his church through an intentional process of racial reconciliation more than a decade ago. I brought up the challenge before me and asked for any advice he might have for me.

I will never forget the simple question he asked me in response, "Have you preached on it before?" I was pierced to the heart. Why? Because in the 12-and-a-half-year history of Preston Trail, I had never spoken about race or racism. The sin of racism, asserting and acting on the assumption that one's race is superior to others, is a sin that for centuries has deeply separated many of God's children. It has helped institutionalize poverty and diminish God's reputation in this world. How does that not even get a mention from me? My job as a spiritual leader is to remind God's people of God's views on the most important things in life. But when it comes to race and racism, I've been AWOL—guilty at best of benign neglect and at worst, spiritual malpractice.

This realization was the catalyst in my own life to begin thinking in new ways about systemic racism, to expand my circle of friendship to include people of different races, and finally to begin working intentionally to bring racial reconciliation to the world in which

I live. It is out of this new way of thinking that I now want to make the turn to helping you know how to guide your children to reflect the character of Jesus in their increasingly multicultural world.

## Helping Your Children Love All the Children of the World

As you begin to shape your child's thoughts about people who are different from them, whether racially, religiously, or socioeconomically, it is important to hold up to them the clear teachings of Jesus about how we are to relate to all people—those who are like us and those who are very different from us. The classic text that lays out Jesus's view is Luke 10:25-37. We can sum up Jesus's teaching with these three phrases:

- Love God.
- Love your neighbor.
- Everyone is your neighbor.

In verses 25-28, Jesus has an encounter with a religious expert.

> One day an expert in religious law stood up to test Jesus by asking him this question:
> "Teacher, what should I do to inherit eternal life?"
> Jesus replied, "What does the law of Moses say? How do you read it?"
> The man answered, "'You must love the LORD your God with all your heart, all your soul, all your strength, and all your mind.' And, 'Love your neighbor as yourself.'"
> "Right!" Jesus told him. "Do this and you will live!" (NLT).

This brief segment of what would become a longer conversation establishes what has come to be known as the Great Commandment—love God and love your neighbor. One of the best gifts you can give your children is to help them understand the true meaning of love at a very early age. So let's take a moment and talk about the kind of love Jesus has in mind when he calls us to love God with our whole hearts and our neighbors as we love ourselves.

### Help your kids love like Jesus.

When it comes to love, the English language is not nearly as expressive as the Greek, in which the New Testament was originally written. English forces us to do a verbal mash-up and use a single word to describe different kinds of love. Where I live, we would say we love Dr. Pepper, the Dallas Cowboys, our spouses, and God. Clearly the word "love" expresses a different nuance in each case. New Testament Greek uses one word to describe the love we have for friends, a different one to describe the love a family shares, and still another to describe romantic love. The word Jesus uses to describe the love we should have for God, our neighbor, and ourselves is different from all three of the above.

The kind of love Jesus refers to is the choice to always work for the very best of another person, even if it requires a lot of effort and even when the person doesn't seem to deserve that kind of love. The transliterated Greek is *agape*, and it is the kind of love God has for us, his children. You can share with your children from their earliest days that God loves them not because they have been good and have done nice things but because that's who God is, a loving God who is like the very best Father. He even continues to love us when we do things that make us unlovable. The perfect picture of this love is our heavenly Father's willingness to allow his own Son, Jesus, to come to earth, live in a human body, and eventually suffer and endure the cross so we can be saved.

As you help your children understand that showing Jesus's kind of love is a choice, they will be relieved to find out that this kind of love does not mean that they have to "like" everyone God wants them to love or that they will feel strong positive emotions toward that person. In fact, Jesus tells us that what distinguishes his kind of love most is when we love our enemies. So when it's time to have the talk with your child about how he can love the class bully, you can talk through how he can work for what is best for the bully without the added pressure of him thinking he has to like him or have positive feelings toward him. You might want to give him a heads-up, though, that if he starts praying for and acting toward the bully in a loving way, God may one day help turn his rival into a friend he can grow to like a lot!

## Help your kids love who Jesus loves.

The religious scribe asks a natural follow-up question: "And who is my neighbor?" Jesus responds with one of his most beloved and memorable stories, the parable of the good Samaritan. A man on the treacherous road to Jericho is robbed, beaten, and left for dead by thieves. Two other Jews who are on the temple payroll see him but pass by on the other side of the road, leaving him for dead. But when a despised Samaritan sees him, he stops—and at his own risk begins to offer assistance. He pulls out his flasks of wine and oil and pours them on the man's wounds to soothe them. He bandages the wounds, takes the bludgeoned man to an inn in Jericho, and pays for the inn-keeper to continue to care for him.

Don't miss what Jesus does in this story. He makes the despised Samaritan—the last person any Jew would consider his or her neighbor—the hero. And what does the Samaritan do for this beaten and bloodied Jew, who is culturally, religiously, and racially different from him and even hostile toward him? He cares for him. He loves him as he would love himself. He considers him to be his neighbor. With great clarity, Jesus is proclaiming that those who follow him will understand that everyone is our neighbor. Jesus's imperative for human relationships bears repeating:

- Love God.
- Love your neighbor.
- Everyone is your neighbor.

As your kids prepare to go to school, where they will meet and become friends with a new and diverse group of kids, it will be helpful for you to have multiple conversations that include a little game you can call Who's Your Neighbor? Describe with appropriate language the various kids they will see and experience, and let them confirm that yes, they are their neighbors.

"How about the kids who seem really smart? Are they your neighbors?"

"How about the kids who struggle a little bit to learn? Are they your neighbors?"

"What about the African American girl who sits two rows over from you? Is she your neighbor?"

"And the Hispanic boy who struggles with English? Is he your neighbor?"

"What about the kid who is harassed by the class bully? Is he your neighbor?"

"What about the class bully himself? Is he your neighbor?"

"What about the classmate with cerebral palsy who is restricted to a wheelchair? Is she your neighbor?"

"What about the popular kids? Are they your neighbors?"

"What about the Muslim family that keeps to themselves? Are they your neighbors?"

Rehearsing this kind of conversation with your children as they move from grade to grade and from challenging situation to challenging situation will help reinforce in their hearts that, indeed, everyone is their neighbor.

*Help your kids reach out to kids who are different from them.*

One of the remarkable things about Jesus is that you can see a pattern of intentionality in his efforts to connect with people who were not the stereotypical practicing Jews of his time. The beloved story in John 4 about Jesus's encounter with a Samaritan woman is a clear illustration. In the narrative, Jesus meets a woman at the well out-side of her town, but we often miss a little phrase that reveals exactly what Jesus is plotting. Verse 4 reads, "Now he had to go through Samaria." This was highly unusual. The Jews regularly took the long way around from Judea to Galilee so they could bypass the hated Samaritans. Have you ever wondered why he had to go through Samaria? Did his advance man tell him he needed to take the shortcut through Samaria so he wouldn't be late to his next speaking engage-ment in Capernaum?

I don't think so. I suggest it was the Spirit that led him to go to Sychar, where he would meet the woman at the well. And maybe, just maybe, the Spirit of God is leading you too...to walk across the room and introduce yourself to a person of color or a person from an ethnic background that's different from yours. Just like Jesus did.

The best way to help your children intentionally build multicul-tural friendships is to let them see you modeling this commitment in your own circle of relationships. Truth be told, after your children begin their schooling, they may become much more open to chil-dren of other races and backgrounds than you are. If this is the case, it will be important for you to affirm their growth in this area and find ways to reinforce it. This is easily done by including children of dif-ferent races or backgrounds in every social occasion you can. Birthday parties, sleepovers, and summer outings are just a few of the oppor-tunities you can leverage to help inculcate this value into your chil-dren's hearts and minds.

This can be intimidating, especially if you have lived a racially insular life. It will feel awkward. You will probably say something wrong or not do everything exactly right. Don't let that stop you. Most people who live as a minority are quick to forgive people who genuinely reach out to them. If you say or do something embarrass-ing, you'll get over it soon enough, and then you'll have a great story to share.

If you need any more motivation to lead your children in this direction, keep in mind that by helping them grow up in a racially diverse environment, you will be setting them up to succeed in almost every area of life going forward. Racial and ethnic diversity is a growing reality. To help your children learn how to embrace and respect people who are different from themselves is to prepare them to live in the brave new world awaiting them.

*Help your kids treat others the way they want to be treated.*

It sounds so elementary—"Do to others whatever you would like them to do to you. This is the essence of all that is taught in the law and the prophets" (Matthew 7:12 NLT). But it may be the single most important principle required to build bridges and establish genuine relationships and friendships with anyone, including those that cross racial and ethnic lines. It's not called the Golden Rule for nothing. It is tucked neatly into the greatest sermon ever preached. Stop and think for just a moment. How do you want to be treated?

- Do you want to be respected? Respect other people.
- Do you want people to listen to you and know your story? Ask them about theirs and listen intently.
- Do you want people to be kind and understanding to you? Be kind and understanding first.
- Do you want to be accepted? Be accepting.

I would think that most thoughtful parents teach their kids the Golden Rule at some point in their early years of development. That is good. However, I have noticed that we confuse the profoundly simple and the profoundly simplistic. Teaching our kids the Golden Rule at an early age feels age appropriate. But when they grow into their teen years and relational decisions get increasingly complex, we might not be so quick to turn to this lesson. It feels a bit trifling to remind your eleventh grader to keep the Golden Rule while they are out on a date or hanging overnight with their friends. It feels a bit simplistic at that stage.

The problem may not be the principle, but our failure to continually update its use and application in our children's lives as they grow older. It is significant that this principle appears in some form in many religions other than Christianity, including Buddhism, Hinduism, Islam, Baha'i, Confucianism, and Jainism. Profoundly *simplistic* principles don't translate across diverse cultures or last for millennia. This universal teaching is hanging around because it is profoundly *simple*.

So throughout your children's development, spin out new applications of this principle that are appropriate for their age and stage.

- When they are in preschool, it's helpful for them to see that when they share their toys with others, others will share with them.
- When they get to elementary school, they will do well not to make fun of and mock kids who are socially awkward, because when they get to middle school, they will be the socially awkward ones and will appreciate catching a break from the older kids.
- When they are in high school and belonging becomes increasingly important, including others who are racially and ethnically different from them will help create an environment where they will feel welcome as well.

If you can both inculcate this time-honored principle into your child's heart and teach them how to use and apply it in multiple situations in their lives, you will have equipped them to be a true relational leader in the places to which God will call them in the future.

## Concluding Thoughts

As I have been working through this chapter, the issues of race, immigration, and sexual identity have been roiling in the background because of significant events unfolding in our country and around the world. The thoughts and principles I've outlined here will become even more crucial in a world that often feels like it is coming apart at the seams because of the surge of globalization. As you talk with your children about racial prejudice, police brutality that appears to be racially motivated, illegal immigration, and the growing prevalence of LGBTQ issues, you will struggle to feel up to the task of speaking intelligibly into their lives. We all feel that way.

That is why I want you to look at the principles in this chapter primarily as a way of thinking. It is apparent to all close observers of the human experience that the way we think shapes who we become. And the way we think, combined with who we have become, determines what we do. You will not be able to be with your children in most of the crucial moments of their lives, but if you have taught them how to love like Jesus, love who Jesus loves, be intentional in their loving, and love others as they desire to be loved, you will have raised peacemakers and kingdom shapers who will be an eternal legacy of your own faith.

...................................................................................

*Dear Lord,*

*In this world, where racial prejudice and strife seem ever present, we need your peace and love to increasingly reign. I fully acknowledge that of all the hearts darkened by this sin, the only one I can control is my own. So, Lord, cleanse me. Forgive me. Help me see everyone, no matter our differences, as fellow brothers and sisters created in your image—and of enough value to you that you would give your Son to ransom them too. And may my example of love and acceptance flow down to my children and my children's children.*

*Amen.*

## Breaking It Down for Every Age

Depending on your own racial and ethnic background, the issues discussed in this chapter may or may not resonate with a sense of urgency. If issues of race don't feel like vital topics you must talk with your kids about, it's important to remember that they are. Our country is grappling with this topic in highly charged, visible ways, and it's important for us to take it up in our homes as well. This is an issue that gets to the very heart of Jesus's teaching: Love God and love others.

### Elementary-Aged Kids

Engage your school-aged kids in conversations about what it means to be a good neighbor. As concrete thinkers, kids will likely assume "neighbor" simply means the handful of people who live in close proximity to your home. Help them expand their understanding of neighbor to anyone who crosses their path, including those who are harder to love or even like. Whether your kids love to read or be read to, seek out age-appropriate books that deal with themes of racism, prejudice, and racial reconciliation (you can easily find a list of award-winning and recommended books on Amazon or at your local library). As they read, ask your kids questions about what they're learning.

### Tweens

As your kids move into their preteen years, help them to identify and think critically about racial stereotypes. If your tween says something that supports a stereotypical mindset, it can be instinctive to shut them down with a sharp "Don't say that!" Instead, ask questions. "Why did you say that?" "What makes you assume that's true?" "How would you feel if someone made that assumption about you?"

## Teens

As your kids grow into their teen years, talk to them about the concept of implicit bias. We have seen that we are easily lulled into the faulty thinking that if we aren't racist, we don't need to do anything about racism. But the reality is that most of us are blind to our implicit racial biases—the unconscious ways we assign stereotypes to other people and judge them accordingly. It is important during these years, perhaps more than at any other stage of their development, to be honest and open with your child about your own implicit biases. This won't damage your credibility; in fact, hearing you share the ways you struggle in this area can go a long way toward earning your teen's respect. Use current events to prompt discussions with your teen about racism in our country and in our own ways of thinking, and encourage them to continue to process these events together with you.

## Questions for Personal Reflection or Group Discussion

1. When you see examples of racism in the media or in real life, what is the first thing that comes to your mind?
2. As you read about the struggle we all have with inherent biases, which assumption did you resonate with most and why?
3. Which definition of love is most prevalent in your family's life? Is it considered more a feeling or an action? How can you help your children practice love as a choice?
4. In practice, not in theory, are there any neighbors who are excluded in your family's conversations and interactions?
5. If you were to develop a meaningful friendship with a person of another race, who would it be? Can you name them? What would be the first step you could take to build that relationship?

## Additional Resources

If you are interested in further reading on this subject, these resources may be helpful.

### For Parents

*More Than Equals* by Spencer Perkins and Chris Rice

*One Body, One Spirit* by George Yancey

*Same Kind of Different as Me* by Ron Hall and Denver Moore

### For Teens

*The Bluest Eye* by Toni Morrison

*To Kill a Mockingbird* by Harper Lee

# 7

# Why Bad Things Happen

## Paul Basden

I was 27 years old when I first had to tell one of my children about why bad things happen.

My wife and I married young, at the age of 22. We both came from homes where faith was important, and our parents left us legacies of unselfish love. We pictured a bright future together with friends, family, church, and work consuming our days. For the first few years, this dream came true. We were learning to love each other as husband and wife, we were grateful for our jobs, and we were looking forward to starting our family. In year three of our marriage, God blessed us with our firstborn, a daughter who wrapped me around her little finger the moment I held her in the hospital room. We liked parenting so much that we wanted another child soon.

Two years later my wife was pregnant with our second child. When our little boy was born, he weighed in at over eight pounds and was more than 20 inches long. The only problem was that he entered the world lifeless. He was in the womb nine full months and emerged fully developed, but he was stillborn. The only son we would bring into the world would never be ours to hold, cuddle, feed, fall in love with, and raise to maturity.

As debilitating as this loss was to my wife and me, we had a three-year-old little girl who would experience it as well. Somehow we needed to break the news to her. As I thought through the uncomfortable conversation before me, I hoped she wouldn't remember much of it because of her young age. That thought comforted me because I had never faced this situation before. True, I had lost my father to a heart attack when I was thirteen years old. But that seemed like ancient history, and I couldn't remember anything my mom said at the time. I now had a little daughter to talk to, and I knew it would be a difficult discussion.

So armed with more courage than wisdom, I came home from the hospital the day of the stillbirth, walked out to the backyard with my three-year-old, and began to explain why she would never meet her new baby brother. I said something like this:

> Mommy had her baby today. It was a little boy…but something went wrong when he was in Mommy's tummy. We don't know what it was, but it was not good. The baby did not live…our doctor told us that if the baby can't live in Mommy's tummy, which is the safest place to grow, then he could never survive in the outside world. I'm sorry to say we won't be bringing your little brother home from the hospital…in a few days we will have a service for him and bury his body. Mommy and I hope we can have another baby soon but not right now. We are all very sad…if you get sad, please talk to us about it. I love you so much.

The real conversation was more dialogue than monologue, but those were my main talking points. My daughter cried a little but didn't have a meltdown. Two years later God blessed us with another child, this time living and breathing.

In many ways, I lucked out. Our daughter was so young that she was not overly impacted by the loss. Nor did she ever see her little brother's lifeless body, which meant there were no haunting memories to frighten her. Yet that daddy-daughter talk remains one of the hardest things I've ever had to do as a parent.

You may have faced a similar situation. Perhaps you too have had to sit down with your child to talk about why bad things happen. The issue might have been up close and personal, like the death of a grandparent. Or it might have been remote but still scary, like what happened at the most recent school shooting. And if you haven't had these conversations with your children yet, you undoubtedly will. Why? Because bad things happen. They are part of life.

Perhaps the most difficult question children ask their parents is why bad things happen. This is not just a tough question—it is a profoundly theological question. That is, it requires us to talk about God. (The word "theology" comes from the Greek *theos* [God] and *logos* [talk].) When this subject surfaces, we usually have two options: We make a lame effort to defend God, or we mumble about how some mysteries just can't be solved. Either way, we have not served our children well.

In this chapter, we offer a helpful answer to why bad things happen. We embrace a biblical perspective and use a format that will help you talk to your kids about this sensitive subject. Don't expect airtight answers to questions that have frustrated the greatest minds throughout history. But you can expect honest and helpful answers to the difficult dilemmas your children face.

## Painting God into a Corner

Like it or not, life contains joys and sorrows, highs and lows, good and bad. You can't have one without the other. As the author of Ecclesiastes makes clear, life is a random rhythm of opposites: birth and death, grief and dance, war and peace. Here is biblical wisdom at its best:

> For everything there is a season,
>     a time for every activity under heaven.
> A time to be born and a time to die.

A time to plant and a time to harvest.
A time to kill and a time to heal.
A time to tear down and a time to build up.
A time to cry and a time to laugh.
A time to grieve and a time to dance.
A time to scatter stones and a time to gather stones.
A time to embrace and a time to turn away.
A time to search and a time to quit searching.
A time to keep and a time to throw away.
A time to tear and a time to mend.
A time to be quiet and a time to speak.
A time to love and a time to hate.
A time for war and a time for peace (Ecclesiastes 3:1-8 NLT).

From this dizzying display of extreme experiences, we can learn a valuable lesson: If we will embrace this irregular arrangement of happiness and unhappiness rather than hope that we can escape all pain and suffering, then we can begin to fathom why bad things happen. This discovery will teach us to trust God in our own darkness, which in turn will help us lead our kids to do the same.

Why do bad things happen? is one of the hardest questions parents and children will ever discuss. It is a challenge to God's character. It paints God into a corner by assuming three truths that are self-contradictory and cannot be resolved: God is good, God is all-powerful, and bad things happen. Yet the question demands resolution.

Any two of these statements can be logically true, but the addition of the third one always leads to a rational dead end. For example...

- If God is good yet bad things happen, then God must not be able to prevent the bad. Conclusion: God is weak.

- If God is all-powerful yet bad things happen, then God must not want to stop them. Conclusion: God is indifferent.

- If God is good and all-powerful, then bad things should not happen, yet they do. Conclusion: God can't be trusted.

Your child may not be thinking through these logical possibilities, but you should know that these shape the discussion. That's why if the problem is framed in this way, any solution will be unsatisfactory to you and to your child. And that's why we parents feel silly or stupid when our kids ask this question and all we can do is stammer and stutter.

But even though there is no airtight response, we must not remain silent. There are good answers to offer. Here are four important things you can say to your children that will guide them through this thorny topic.

## God Is Good

Affirm the biblical truths that good comes from God alone and nothing evil comes from God. Here are two Scripture passages you may want to read with your kids:

- "God cannot be tempted by evil, nor does he tempt anyone…Every good and perfect gift is from above, coming down from the Father" (James 1:13,17).
- "God is light; in him there is no darkness at all" (1 John 1:5).

Children need to know that God is not the author of evil, that God does not cause bad things. But don't settle for pointing your kids to an abstract God in heaven who is theoretically good. Instead, go straight to the concrete life of Jesus on earth. The testimony of first-century eyewitnesses was that "Jesus went around doing good" (Acts 10:38 NLT). Show your kids that because Jesus is good, we can know that God is good. Remind them that Jesus is the perfect picture of God.

- "Christ is the visible image of the invisible God" (Colossians 1:15 NLT).
- "The Son radiates God's own glory and expresses the very character of God" (Hebrews 1:3 NLT).

I grew up in a home where we prayed, read the Bible, and attended church faithfully—yet I didn't understand that Jesus was the face of God. Although I had been baptized at the age of ten, my knowledge of God was theoretical, impersonal, and secondhand. But in January 1972, at the age of sixteen, I had a spiritual encounter with Jesus Christ that altered the course of my life. Soon after that, I heard about a huge weeklong Jesus festival in Texas—Explo '72. Its goal was to bring together 100,000 high school and college students to inspire and train them to share their faith. Although I lived 1,300 miles from Dallas, I felt compelled to attend. Two friends and I made the long drive from Richmond, Virginia, to Dallas.

The festival lived up to its hype. On the final night, Billy Graham gave the closing message, and I can still remember something he said in his sermon: "When I want to know what God is like, I take a long look at Jesus." That statement became the cornerstone of my maturing theology—God's character is defined most clearly by Jesus.

I think this is the truest thing you can tell your children. When they want to know what God is like, tell them to take a long look at Jesus. They will discover that if God is like Jesus, then God must be good.

Over the years, I've faced my share of trials. The most troubling test has been watching our youngest daughter, now an adult, suffer from a rare genetic disease. For reasons unknown and inexplicable, her chromosomal spelling got scrambled at conception. The symptoms were not obvious at first, but in her 30-plus years of life, she has suffered more pain than most people I know. Both of her hips have been replaced with artificial balls and sockets, her back has been fused from pelvis to shoulders, and her wrist and ankle are partially fused. Her bones break easily, and she takes multiple medications to alleviate her daily discomfort. Her internal thermostat is out of whack, so she doesn't sweat—which means hot weather exposes her to the risk of heatstroke. Her emotional margin is razor thin as she lives in fear that something else will break down soon. Despite her best intentions and our best efforts, our daughter finds herself disabled.

My wife and I have often struggled to know what and how to pray for her. At times we've wondered, "God, do you hear our prayers? Will we ever see her get better? Should we stop praying if the dice have been cast and her condition is irreversible?" One day I found myself being unusually blunt with the Lord in prayer.

> God, I've been praying for my daughter's healing for decades. Yet she seems to be getting worse! Truthfully, if it weren't for Jesus, I don't know that I could keep trusting you. If it weren't for Jesus, I don't know if I could really love you. If it weren't for Jesus, I might quit you.
>
> But...I believe that you have revealed your true self in the face of your Son. I believe that your Son is the perfect picture of you. Therefore, I also believe that down deep, whether I see it or not, you are truly good. So I will keep trusting you. I won't give up on you. I won't quit you.

When issues of evil and suffering lead to questions about the character of God, remember that Jesus is proof that God is good. Help your children grasp God's love as demonstrated in Christ.

- "You see, at just the right time, when we were still powerless, Christ died for the ungodly. Very rarely will anyone die for a righteous person, though for a good person someone might possibly dare to die. But God demonstrates his own love for us in this: While we were still sinners, Christ died for us" (Romans 5:6-8).

- "This is how God showed his love among us: He sent his one and only Son into the world that we might live through him. This is love: not that we loved God, but that he loved us and sent his Son as an atoning sacrifice for our sins" (1 John 4:9-10).

The full picture of God's love is always Jesus. At times, that may be the only thing that will keep you from doubting the character of God. When bad things happen, let this confidence help you lead your family through this toughest of topics.

## Life Has Ups and Downs

This is where you can clarify that bad things come in two categories: human evil and natural evil. There's a difference.

Human evil is seen when one person does a bad thing to another person. This is what lies behind bullying in our schools, abuse in our homes, and crime in our streets. The Bible is filled with examples of human evil. Cain kills Abel out of jealousy, David seduces Bathsheba out of lust, and Judas betrays Jesus out of greed. The common denominator in each story is that a person uses freedom of choice to get what they want, even if it means harming another person in the process. This is what we mean by human evil.

As we know from Genesis 1–2, God made humans good and created them in his image. Part of being created in God's image means that we have the freedom to say yes or no to God and to God's ways. Had God made us robots, we could only say yes. But because God made us free to choose, we can say yes or no. Sadly, people have chosen to say no to God too often. When we misuse our free will and choose evil over good, we are making evil choices. The result? Others suffer the sad consequences of our sinful actions.

Your kids probably don't follow traditional news outlets, but they are exposed to a constant stream of disturbing information. They know that teens take their lives in school hallways. They know that parents abuse their kids. They know that terrorists behead their enemies halfway around the world. You can help bring mental order to your child's chaotic thinking by explaining that these are all abuses of our God-given freedom. Remind them that to create a world where nobody does evil, God would have to forbid human freedom. He has chosen not to do that so we can freely choose to love him. Bottom line: Human evil is the price we pay for freedom.

Natural evil is different. You see it when random events in nature hurt people. The Ebola outbreak in West Africa is an example. So are Hurricane Harvey and breast cancer. Although human choice was not the culprit, suffering still happened.

Explain to your children that human sin has corrupted not only human choices but also the natural world. That is, both natural evil and human evil can be traced back to the abuse of our free will. Here is how the apostle Paul grappled with this idea.

> Against its will, all creation was subjected to God's curse. But with eager hope, the creation looks forward to the day when it will join God's children in glorious freedom from death and decay. For we know that all creation has been groaning as in the pains of childbirth right up to the present time (Romans 8:20-22 NLT).

By turning our backs on God, we humans caused not just a severe disruption in our relationships with God and others, but a radical disruption in nature as well. It is this last consequence, disorder in nature, that comes into focus here. Nature has somehow suffered because of our sinful rebellion, and we are not immune from its agony. This mystery is not explained anywhere in the Bible—certainly not to the satisfaction of us scientific Westerners, who are linear and logical in our worldview.

All we can say, based on the belief that Jesus is the perfect picture of God, is that God did not intend viruses to wipe out villages, mosquitoes to kill innocent bystanders, or rapidly reproducing cells to morph into malignant cancer. This is not God's will. It is the sad consequence of living in a fallen world that has been tainted by human sin.

Help your child understand that since everyone is a sinner (Romans 3:23) and sin always brings death (Romans 6:23), everyone is going to die at some point and also suffer along the way. No one is exempt. Pointing to the inevitability of pain and death in this world, a wise sage once said, "We were born crying, we will die crying, and in between we will cry some more." Natural evil is the cause of many of these tears.

Philip Yancey, in his book *Disappointment with God*, tells the story of a friend whom he refers to as George. For years George had known a relatively easy existence, but through an unexpected series of events, his life took a tragic turn. One day his wife was diagnosed with advanced metastatic breast cancer. They were in shock. For the next several months she faced chemotherapy and radiation routines bravely with him at her side.

While this was going on, another tragedy occurred. George and his daughter were in a serious car wreck caused by a drunk driver. George incurred a brain injury that initially caused severe vision problems and chronic headaches and ultimately so disabled him that even the simple task of eating a meal became a chore.

One day Philip met George for breakfast and asked the poignant question, "How has God disappointed you?"

To Philip's astonishment, George answered that he was not upset with God. When Philip asked how that could be possible, George answered, "I learned not to confuse God with life."[1]

Tell your kids that life has ups and downs, but life and God are not identical. They don't need to confuse life with God. When they experience hurt or pain, help them avoid the line of reasoning that says, "I am really hurting, but I am not the cause of my pain. If I didn't cause it, then someone else did. Since I don't know anyone else to blame it on, God must have caused it. I could never love or trust this kind of God!" This is what happens when people confuse God with life. This may also be why so many angry atheists hate a divine being they don't even believe exists.

To sum up, if your children refuse to confuse God with life, they will understand that God is good, that life has both good and bad, and that human and natural evil are behind all that is bad. It's a sign of maturity when your child comes to accept that life has ups and downs because we inhabit a fallen world.

## God Uses Bad Things for Good Purposes

At the heart of Christianity lies the conviction that God transforms evil into good. After all, he used the gruesome murder of the best man who ever lived to reconcile the world to himself. So you're on firm footing when you tell your child that God has the power to use bad things for good purposes.

But you must be crystal clear, or you will be miserably misunderstood. You're not saying that God causes everything, you're not saying that everything is good, and you're not saying that suffering is good. In fact, you're saying that God does not cause evil of any kind, that suffering is never good in and of itself, and that it is never wise to minimize evil by calling it good.

What you are saying is that God, in his power and creativity, knows how to exploit evil for his redemptive purposes. He specializes in bringing order out of chaos, meaning out of emptiness, and good out of bad. Not only is this principle true in the case of Jesus, but it is true for all who trust God. "We know that God causes everything to work together for the good of those who love God and are called according to his purpose for them" (Romans 8:28 NLT).

God is not willing for evil to have the last word, so in love and mercy he takes our bad experiences and morphs them into our maturity if we will trust him.

You can't expect younger children to understand this abstract concept, but you can tell them a story that illustrates this idea in action. Tell them the story of Joseph, found in Genesis 37–50.

Joseph grew up as the favorite son of his father, Jacob. That wouldn't have been a big deal had he been an only child, but Joseph had ten brothers, and they got really tired of Joseph receiving the royal treatment at home. They weren't too fond of his bigheaded bragging either.

One day the brothers got so sick of Joseph, they were ready to kill him. On further reflection, they decided that might be a little harsh, so they sold him into slavery and sent him off to the faraway land of Egypt.

While Joseph was there, he suffered greatly. He was lonely, mistreated as a slave, and in and out of prison. Yet he never lost faith in God, nor did God ever forget Joseph.

By the time he was an adult, Joseph had risen to the height of political power and was second in authority only to the Pharaoh himself. When a severe famine struck the Middle East, Jacob sent his sons down to Egypt to buy grain so his family wouldn't starve. In a providential turn of events, the brothers had to appear before Joseph to beg for grain. What irony! The men who had sold their younger brother into slavery years ago were now bowing before him, begging for their lives. And they had no idea who he was.

It didn't take Joseph long to recognize his brothers or to decide how to treat them. Because God had been so good to him, he decided he would be good to them. What Joseph finally told them points to the divine mystery behind this principle: "You intended to harm me, but God intended it all for good. He brought me to this position so I could save the lives of many people" (Genesis 50:20 NLT).

By the grace of God, Joseph came to see that what his brothers did was indeed evil…yet God was able to use it for good.

As you share the story of Joseph with your children, you can go even further. God not only uses bad things for good purposes in our lives but also uses those bad things, when redeemed, to help others make it through their bad experiences. That is what the apostle Paul meant when he wrote, "Praise be to the God and Father of our Lord Jesus Christ, the Father of compassion and the God of all comfort, who comforts us in all our troubles, so that we can comfort those in any trouble with the comfort we ourselves receive from God" (2 Corinthians 1:3-4).

In the words of Pastor Rick Warren, "God never wastes a hurt."

When our daughters were young, one of their favorite babysitters, Laurie, was a young adult in our church. She was loud, fun, and a kid at heart. She also loved our girls, which made us love her.

Laurie married when she was almost 40. She and her husband pictured a great life together, but their "happily ever after" abruptly ended soon after their first wedding anniversary, when Laurie was diagnosed with stage III breast cancer. At the advice of her oncologist, she underwent surgery to remove the malignancy, had a double mastectomy, and entered a one-year regimen of chemotherapy and radiation.

By God's grace, Laurie's cancer has now been in remission for more than a decade. Out of gratitude to God, she has decided to be a good steward of her suffering. She recycles her pain by caring for women with breast cancer. She attends doctor's appointments with them, comforts them while they are receiving chemotherapy, and prays for them faithfully. Cancer is bad, but Laurie refuses to let it ruin her life. She has let God bring good out of it.

God is so big and powerful, he can use even the worst things in life for good ends.

## Bad Things Won't Last Forever

Children love stories with happy endings, so this should be easy for your kids to comprehend. Tell them that what we see now is not how it will always be. Tell them that Jesus will return one day to create new heavens and a new earth, where there will be no more sin and suffering. In that new world, evil and crime and war will disappear; abuse and addiction will be bad dreams from the past; cancer and car wrecks, hurricanes and heart attacks, suicide and self-hatred will all melt away. On that day the love of Christ will be center stage, and we will all have front-row seats. Then we will have the answers to all our questions.

A few years ago, my friend Roger experienced firsthand what it is like to talk to his kids about why bad things happen. He was diagnosed with mantle cell lymphoma, a rare form of cancer. Although surprised at the diagnosis, he said he never really worried. He trusted God for the outcome and was ready to accept life or death. But what would he say to his six children, and how would he say it? He and his wife had always been transparent with their kids about family matters, not keeping secrets or sheltering them from the trials of life. So not long after the diagnosis, he told them about the cancer, the chemotherapy, and the impact on the family.

His youngest daughter, who was ten years old at the time, struggled with the news more than the others. Unlike her siblings, she was not old enough to visit her dad in the hospital while he was being treated. That made her anxious. For comfort, she purchased a stuffed animal and named it Beatrice. But she didn't keep it for herself— she asked her dad to take Beatrice to the cancer ward. Through Beatrice, she could be with her dad vicariously. When he talked to her via FaceTime, he held Beatrice in his arms so she could see the doll. This made her feel like she could be present during his time of difficulty, even if not in person.

Roger told his kids the truth. He explained that God is good, even when bad things happen, and he helped them learn to trust this good God. You can do the same with your children.

As you and your children face this difficult topic of why bad things happen, may this prayer turn your attention to the One who suffered for us, that our sufferings might be redeemed.

..................................................................................

*Dear Jesus,*

*The suffering servant of Isaiah 53 is described as a man of sorrows, acquainted with grief. That prophecy was pointing to you. That's not what any of us expected the Messiah and Son of God to be. We expected a man of comfort, acquainted with joys. But to save us, you became one of us, entering*

*fully into our human experience. You tasted the ups
and downs, the highs and lows, the good and bad
that come with humanity. .Because you share our
humanity, we understand you better—and we dare
to believe that you understand us better. As humans,
we all know sorrow and are acquainted with grief.
Help us find you amid the bad so we can trust you to
turn it into something good.*

*Amen.*

## Breaking It Down for Every Age

Helping your kids grapple with this age-old question of why bad things happen to good people is no small task. Ultimately, it is an opportunity to help your children come to terms with the nature of the world around them and the good God who created it and is at work redeeming it. Here are some thoughts to keep in mind as you address this topic during different stages of your child's growth.

### Elementary-Aged Kids

When your child comes to you with questions about the bad things that happen in the world around him, point to two principles shared in this chapter: God is good, and life has ups and downs. As you help him reconcile these two realities, you may want to point to the truth articulated by the gentle and genial Fred Rogers of TV's *Mr. Rogers' Neighborhood*. Whenever bad things happened, he said, his mother taught him, "Look for the helpers. You will always find people who are helping." Help your kids understand that our good God weeps with those who weep in the down times of life, and he is often seeking to comfort them through helping people. Encourage your kids to identify opportunities to be the helper in someone else's life when others are facing bad things.

### Tweens

As your kids reach the preteen years, it will be increasingly difficult to shield them from the harsher realities of our sinful world. As they become more aware of the tragedies that rock the lives of innocent people, help them understand the impact of sin on our world. When your tween comes to you with questions about the bad things in life, assure her that bad things are never from God. Bad things are the result of either human evil or natural evil. Emphasize God's goodness, and find opportunities in your own life to tell of God's ability to bring good purposes out of bad things.

### Teens

The teen years are a crucial time for faith to become personal in your child's life. Your willingness to help him process the tough question of why bad things happen to good people will go a long way toward establishing a firm foundation for adult faith. Let him ask questions, express confusion and sorrow, and even be angry at God. He can handle it. As you help your teen think through this difficult issue, he will doubtless have questions that defy easy answers. Perhaps the most helpful truth to consistently point him back to is that God's character is defined most clearly in Jesus. In the face of all the things we can't reconcile about God's sovereignty and life's brokenness, help him understand that we can place our faith in God's character because of who he is revealed to be in Jesus Christ.

## Questions for Personal Reflection or Group Discussion

1. Have your children faced a painful experience in life yet? If so, did they talk to you about it? Why or why not?
2. What bad thing in your life has caused you sorrow or resentment? How has it impacted your relationship to God?
3. "I learned not to confuse God with life." So said Philip Yancey's

friend who was in constant pain. How can that insight help you grow through past hurts you have faced?

4. How do Bible stories of people who suffered—especially Joseph and Jesus—help you understand God's power to redeem bad things? How much have you told your children about these stories?

## Additional Resources

If you are interested in further reading on this subject, these resources may be helpful.

### For Parents

"Making Sense Out of Suffering" by Peter Kreeft, in *Life, God, and Other Small Topics*, edited by Eric Metaxas

*The Problem of Pain* by C.S. Lewis

*The Reason for God* by Tim Keller (chapters 2, 10, 12)

### For Children and Teens

*Case for Faith for Kids* by Lee Strobel (chapter 1)

*The Case for Faith Student Edition* by Lee Strobel (chapter 1)

# 8

# Porn

### Jim Johnson

'm not usually an alarmist, but when it comes to the pervasive presence of pornography in our culture and its druglike power to abduct the hearts and minds of our children, I say sound them all! In fact, I believe this issue may be the most likely to negatively impact your children, the most difficult to shield your children from, and the most intractable to free them from if they fall victim to its addictive grip.

If you need a wake-up call, just let the title of this article posted by Fight the New Drug sink in for a minute: "Sex Before Kissing: How 15-Year-Old Girls Are Dealing with Porn-Addicted Boys." The main point of the article is that teenage boys addicted to porn have developed a view about sex that is totally disconnected from intimacy. So girls, in order to please their boyfriends, perform sex acts on them so they can get on to doing more normal adolescent things like kissing. This quote from the article is chillingly telling.

> When asked, "How do you know a guy likes you?" an 8th grade girl replied: "He still wants to talk to you after you [give him oral sex]." A male high school student said to a girl: "If you [give me oral sex] I'll give you a kiss." Girls are

expected to provide sex acts for tokens of affection, and are coached through it by porn-taught boys. A 15-year-old girl said she didn't enjoy sex at all, but that getting it out of the way quickly was the only way her boyfriend would stop pressuring her and watch a movie.[1]

If you are like me, you're probably asking, how did we get here? What factors have come into play in our families and culture that could create such a disconcerting reality? As I observe the current machinations of modern life, I see five dynamic forces at work that are creating an erotic elixir that threatens the physical, relational, and spiritual well-being of our children.

- the natural curiosity children have about sexuality and sex
- the hormonal rush of puberty
- the pervasive presence of sexual imagery and innuendo in our culture
- the easy accessibility of hard-core pornography on the internet and social media
- pornography's power to chemically hijack and alter young, developing brains

Taken together, these five forces exert a powerful influence over the minds and hearts of our children. Even now as I look at the five factors above, it is sobering to see that as a parent, I have very little control over them. With rare exceptions, every little boy is going to be fascinated with his penis and wonder what it can do. Every little girl will ask why she doesn't have one and then marvel one day at her own developing breasts. Puberty is about as sure as death and taxes, and it only serves to ratchet up the questions that most of us have been asked (but that in good taste I will refrain from including here). Sex sells in our culture, and the billion-dollar porn industry is doing everything it can to capitalize on that fact. It is not going away. All the while, our children who see a plethora of sexual images or view hard-core pornography at an increasingly early age are at the mercy of how their habit-prone brains are wired to function. The complexity of this issue tempts us to bury our heads in the sand and simply hope it will go away. But the compelling demand of parental love challenges us to face it head-on.

As your kids grow, your ability to manage the dual functions of protecting your children from pornography and preparing them to deal with it will be severely tested. The struggle is intense, particularly because of two of the factors we mentioned above—the accessibility of porn and its impact on brain chemistry. Before we can chart out an effective strategy to help our kids overcome this enemy of true intimacy, we need to have a clear idea of what we are up against.

## Modern-Day Porn

Modern-day porn is not your grandfather's pornography. My first exposure to porn occurred when I was in third grade—about 1964. I lived on the outskirts of Midland, Texas. Across the street from my subdivision was flat desert as far as the eye could see. One afternoon, a friend of mine and I were exploring the desert. About 15 or 20 minutes in, we found a fort that some other kids had built. Now, by fort, I'm referring to a hole dug in the ground and covered with plywood to create a little place to hide.

We started poking around a bit and found a weathered and tattered magazine with a picture of a bunny on the front—a different kind of bunny than I had ever seen. Only recently had we heard of a magazine called *Playboy*, and we thought we had discovered a kind of illicit pure gold. We brushed the West Texas sand off the pictures, and needless to say, what we saw enlightened the curiosity of a couple of nine-year-olds. The women were beautiful, scantily clad in most pictures, and topless in the centerfold.

My friend and I went back into the desert a couple more times that year to check out the fort (read: magazine). But as enticing as the *Playboy* was, we had to walk 20 minutes through cactus and mesquite trees, pull it carefully out of a spider-infested hideaway, and brush off gritty sand, only to see the same faded, water-stained pictures of playgirls. Looking back gratefully, I can see that this experience made an indelible impression in my mind that porn just wasn't worth the effort. As a result, I think I was somewhat immunized to the lure of pornography at a young age, and for that reason, I have not had to struggle as much as some against its addictive power.

I shudder to think, though, how much different my experience and life trajectory might be if I were nine years old today. That 20-minute walk would be reduced to 20 seconds as my friend and I would walk into his dad's office and Google "sex" on his unfiltered computer. And we wouldn't be looking at still shots of seemingly innocent young beauties enticing us in various stages of undress. We would see hard-core videos of various sex acts, the majority of which have a violent slant showing women being physically and verbally abused as men exert a dominant hypermasculinity. Male brains of any age, not to mention preteen male brains, cannot watch these images for long and not be negatively impacted.

## What Is Pornography?

Historically, it has been difficult to define exactly what makes porn, porn. A memorable yet not particularly helpful attempt to define pornography was penned by Supreme Court Justice Potter Stewart in *Jacobellis v. Ohio* in 1964, which involved censorship of a movie deemed "obscene." Attempting to explain that the Constitution protected obscenity (aside from hard-core pornography), he wrote, "I shall not today attempt further to define the kinds of material I understand to be embraced within that shorthand description ['hard-core pornography'], and perhaps I could never succeed in intelligibly doing so. But I know it when I see it."[2]

I think it can be said that most of us "know it when we see it." But let's see if we can gain a little more clarity than Justice Stewart offers. The word "pornography" from its Greek roots means "writing about prostitutes." Two implications can be easily drawn from this etymology. First, it is referring to sex that is devoid of relational intimacy or the valuing of the other apart from a business transaction. Second, it is meant to stimulate sexual excitement. From these original sentiments, we might describe something as pornographic if it visually reduces a person to a sexual object for the sexual gratification of others.

When we factor in today's incredibly lucrative and aggressive porn industry, we need to add a new dimension to the definition. Wendy and Larry Maltz, in their book *The Porn Trap*, do just that. They define pornography as "any sexually explicit material that is intended to be, or is used as, a sexual outlet." But they go on to add that the goal of making porn is to "create a connection between the user and the material (usually for the economic benefit of the maker) instead of with a human being."[3] The parenthetical statement captures the driving force behind much of our pornified culture—the greed and profitability of the porn industry, to which we will turn next.

## The Accessibility of Porn

If ever there was a marriage made in hell, it is the marriage of the porn industry and the internet. The internet makes porn ubiquitous. No longer is it limited to the covered rack in your local convenience store or the roadside XXX video outlet. Porn is portable. You can take it with you anywhere and watch it anytime, thanks to the internet.

As a result, pornography is big business—$13 billion annually in the United States and $97 billion annually around the world. These figures do not include mainstream businesses that profit indirectly from the digital distribution of porn under the radar.[4] The upshot of this is that pornography has never been as accessible as it is now. Just to see, I Googled the word "Porn" and 2.12 *billion* websites were aggregated by Google's search engine in .31 seconds. (I didn't click on any of them, by the way, just in case you were wondering.) There is more porn at one's fingertips on the internet than can be watched in a lifetime.

No wonder that the proliferation of computers, smartphones, and tablets has made the average age of a child's first exposure to pornography 11 years old.[5] Young males (12 to 17) are among the most frequent consumers of pornography, and the words "sex" and "porn" were the fourth and fifth most popular searches conducted by children and teens in 2009.[6] Makes you wonder how they would rate today.

Statistics often allow us to keep an issue at arm's length emotionally. But the truth is, it's not a question of *if* your children will be exposed to pornography, but *when*. That's why it's so important that you begin as early as possible to intentionally equip them to respond to this exposure in a healthy and thoughtful way. The stakes get higher as they mature, and the impact of pornography on our children can be dramatic and enduring.

## The Impact of Porn on Children

Recent developments in neuroscience are helping us understand in a clearer way how porn can hijack the minds and hearts of kids as well as adults. We'll consider the impact of porn on anyone who watches it, young or old. The most disconcerting thing, though, is that the brains of children and teens are much more susceptible to the chemical processes that lead to addiction.[7] Pornography impacts an individual in a myriad of ways, but I'm going to highlight the two most significant.

### Porn rewires your kid's brain.

I'm not a neuroscientist. I don't play one on TV, and I have not stayed at a Holiday Inn Express lately. So I'm going to give you a layman's summary of how our brain is impacted by pornography. Each of us has what is called a "reward circuit" in our brains. God designed it to help us survive and thrive in our lives. Whenever we do something that enhances our chances, like eating, bonding with another person, having sex, or even experiencing novelty, the neurons in our brain fire and give us a shot of dopamine and a cocktail of other chemicals that give us a pleasurable feeling meant to reinforce that behavior. Thus a craving is created.

When neurons fire together, they wire together, and a neural pathway is formed. The path is created to make it easier for our reward circuit to release the happy chemicals the next time we do the same behavior. If we return to that behavior again and again, our reward circuit floods our brain with dopamine. Recognizing that this might be a problem, our brain reduces the flow, and we soon notice we aren't getting the same happy feelings. Neuroscientists call this development "tolerance." So now, if we want to experience the same level of pleasurable feelings, we must take our behavior up a notch or two—and addiction is just around the corner.

As helpful as our reward circuit is, it has a flaw. It can't always identify behaviors that are in fact damaging to us. Enter pornography. When your child views pornography, it stimulates their reward circuit in the same manner as bonding with another person or having sex does. The happy chemicals rush in, giving your child a pleasurable feeling that reinforces the behavior. Before long, a strong craving develops, and soon they are logging on and clicking play every chance they get. The more they do, though, the more they develop a tolerance for what they are seeing, and the more graphic and twisted the porn has to be for them to experience the same "high." This explains why kids and adults start viewing things that before would have appalled or shocked them. Even when they stop liking porn, they continue to crave it. Addiction is in the house.[8]

There is a bit of good news in all this. Our brain has plasticity. That means we can let some pathways grow fallow, and with the passing of time, the cravings will subside. This process is helped when we create new pathways by altering our behavior and allowing our reward circuit to create new, healthier cravings. This is the neurological process of breaking old habits and creating new ones. The human brain clearly is one of God's most amazing creations!

*Porn distorts your kid's perceptions about sex and intimacy.*

One of the most troubling aspects of modern-day porn is how violent and brutal it has become. A 2010 study randomly selected 50 of the 250 top-grossing pornographic films of that year. After assessing 304 scenes, they found 3,375 acts of verbal and physical abuse— 11.5 acts of aggression per scene. On the other hand, positive sexual behavior made up just 9.9 percent of all actions.[9] It doesn't take a lot of effort to imagine how viewing this kind of pornography is going to shape a young teenager's perspective on sex and relationships. Here is a brief list of the distorted views and attitudes that are emerging in the minds and hearts of young teens.

- A man's value is determined by his sexual performance, hyper-masculinity, and dominance over women.
- A woman's value is determined by a hypersexualized look and sexual availability.
- Having sex is disconnected from relational commitment or intimacy.
- Sex that is violent and degrading to a woman is normal.
- Sexual novelty (new sexual experiences with new partners) is the norm.

The alarming consequences of developing these distorted views are that children will begin to act them out. Claudine Gallacher, in a blog post for the nonprofit organization Protect Young Minds, shares the tragic story of one nine-year-old boy and how an early and accidental exposure to porn tore his family apart.

> Jason (not his real name) was seven years old when he saw his first pornographic picture. While watching a You-Tube video on his mom's computer, he noticed an explicit advertisement.
> *What's this?*

Click.

Instantly, he was pulled into the world of hard-core pornography. It was an accidental exposure. Jason never intended to start watching porn. But he couldn't stop. And he kept secretly finding more to look at. Unfortunately, his habit went undiscovered for two more years until he was nine. This is when Jason started "acting out" scenes from pornographic videos while "playing" with his younger siblings. He was doing what normal kids do: imitating behavior. Jason's siblings followed his lead. Eventually, his parents caught several of their young kids doing inappropriate things with each other. When the two-year old started exhibiting sexual behavior, his parents needed an answer. But they were not prepared for what came next: Jason confessed to molesting his younger siblings.[10]

As it turns out, Jason's foray into the world of pornography altered his perceptions of sexual behavior to the point that it was deemed unsafe for him to stay in his home. He had to enter a residential treatment center for an extended period to relearn the appropriate ways of touching others. This may sound like something that could never happen to you or anyone you know, but Jason's story is not an isolated incident. The most recent research paints a disturbing picture that children and teens who view violent porn are six times more likely to exhibit sexually aggressive behavior in the future, begin having sex at an earlier age, view sexual violence against women as normal, and engage in risky sexual behavior.[11] Gail Dines, in a widely viewed Ted Talk on this topic, highlights this new reality when she notes punk rock porn star Joanna Angel's comment that up-and-coming young porn stars come to the set "porn ready."[12]

## Do More Than Tell Your Kids About Pornography

Don't be surprised if you're starting to feel a little anxious and sick to your stomach. In light of the cultural onslaught of pornography, it's clear that we must do more than talk about this topic with our kids. What then should our response be? It is here that the Bible can speak words of wisdom, direction, and encouragement to us. Three passages in particular set out a healthy strategy for parents to follow.

The writer of Proverbs clearly articulates the overarching goal of our parenting efforts. "Guard your heart above all else, for it determines the course of your life" (Proverbs 4:23 NLT). The condition of the heart (not the physical one, but the spiritual one, which the Scriptures refer to as the seat of the human will, decision, and emotions) sets the trajectory and tone for our children's lives. As we are learning, this challenge of guarding our children's hearts while they are still in our care is becoming increasingly difficult in the modern world. If we are going to guard our kids' hearts, we need to focus on three biblical principles.

First, for as long as we can, we must protect their eyes. In Jesus's Sermon on the Mount, he reminds us that what we see, what we are exposed to, creates a memorable experience that can impact our growth and development.

> Your eye is like a lamp that provides light for your body. When your eye is healthy, your whole body is filled with light. But when your eye is unhealthy, your whole body is filled with darkness. And if the light you think you have is actually darkness, how deep that darkness is! (Matthew 6:22-23 NLT).

For this reason, then, we will explore how you can protect your children's eyes.

Second, we must train their hearts to make wise decisions. The human heart can be trained—why else would the author of Proverbs write, "Train up a child in the way he should go, even when he is old he will not depart from it" (Proverbs 22:6 NASB)? Some emerging organizations are devoted to helping parents train their children to respond in healthy ways when they are confronted with porn. We will share some of the best practices of these groups that are devoted to protecting children's eyes and hearts.

And finally, we must go beyond protecting our children and also prepare them to overcome this seduction by introducing them to the power of higher affections.[13] This is the ultimate and most powerful antidote to the lure of pornography. As parents, we can protect them only so long before porn breaches the gates of their hearts. When this occurs, their hearts must be full and their sense of purpose must be clear and compelling if they are to slough off the attacks of the evil one and live the kind of life in which there is no room for porn.

### Protect your kid's eyes.

Most experts agree that the older your children are before their first experience of porn, the better. Therefore, hypervigilance in controlling their environment in their preteen years is especially warranted. You will need to set wise technological and relational boundaries in three arenas—your home, your children's extended family and friends, and your children's access to social media through their mobile devices.

When it comes to your home, every technological device is a potential gateway to pornography. You should be aware that your kid quite likely will know more about how to operate your computer, TV, smartphone, tablet, and gaming system than you do. Her curiosity will compel her to explore the far reaches of every device—and that's the problem. That's why it is imperative that you install and monitor every available parental restriction your hardware and software provides.

In *The Tech-Wise Family*, Andy Crouch lines out some helpful everyday steps for "putting technology in its proper place." When it comes to monitoring your kids' devices, Crouch advises,

> The tech-wise family will make a simple commitment to
> one another: no technological secrets, and no place to hide

them…Until children reach adulthood, parents should have total access to their children's devices. I'm well aware this won't stop teenagers from deleting text messages the moment they arrive, relying on self-destructive apps like Snapchat, and engaging in countless other subterfuges— if they choose. But when they do so, they will know they are violating a family practice of openness to and with one another; they will be making choices, even poor ones, within a moral framework rather than simply blundering their way through adolescence without any guidance or boundaries.[14]

What makes this challenge so insidious is that when we think we've got the proper boundaries in place in our own homes, our kids are still vulnerable when they go to the homes of extended family members or friends. Again, every device in those homes is a gateway to porn, including smartphones. The defense line we are trying to set up around our children can become porous very quickly. We are aware of only two strategies you can employ at this juncture.

First, you can become proactive in these extended relationships by allowing your children to visit people's homes only if you have talked with the parents about the boundaries they have in place to keep their homes safe from the intrusion of porn. If any of the parents do not share your concern about this issue and do not have effective restraints in place, take the risk of being the unpopular and over-wrought parents and do not let your child visit there. You will not regret it. It will be worth it in the long run. You can bear the scrutiny and criticism because the stakes are so high.

Second, you can avoid these awkward conversations by creating an environment in your home that draws kids to your place. Do all you can to keep your kids and their friends under the umbrella of the safe place you have created. It may be a little more expensive to have the gaming system du jour, keep the pantry stocked, and have a few unexpected guests at mealtime, but the added costs pale in comparison to the relational damages you will have to repair if your children get hooked on hard-core porn at an early age.

The third venue, and perhaps the most critical one today, is the smartphones we give our children. We are giving them their first phones earlier and earlier. The average age of receiving one's first cell phone has dropped recently from twelve to ten.[15] We do this ostensibly for their safety and security. The fact is, though, that their entanglement with their little block of goodness is opening the door to various kinds of addiction and relational distortion.

A small movement is emerging in which parents are refusing to give their kids smartphones until their midteens.[16] Apps like Instagram and Snapchat are becoming the primary providers for capturing and viewing amateur pornography. The average age sexting begins is now fifth grade.[17] A world of pornography is one click away. Why put your child at risk not just to porn but also to bullying and intense social pressure? The solution a growing number of parents are turning to is a dumbed-down cellphone that can be used only to send and receive texts and place phone calls. This allows parents to observe their children and discern whether they can manage their phone responsibly before they give them one that opens up access to the World Wide Web.

If for some reason you can't refrain from giving your child a fully loaded smartphone, a parental control program like Qustodio can be helpful. This versatile program provides parents access to their children's text messages, blocks certain apps on demand, or even shuts down the phone remotely. Jesse Weinberger, author of *The Boogeyman Exists; and He's in Your Child's Back Pocket*, espouses an attitude that will serve our children well. She reminds us that our only job is to prepare our children for the day they leave. If that's the case, we must be okay with doing and saying things they don't like if that's what it takes to keep them safe.[18]

We recognize this approach may feel draconian and cause an insufferable amount of petitioning if not outright whining. But think and pray long and hard about this. When to give your children their first smartphones may be one of the most important parenting decisions you make. Seek plenty of wise counsel, do your research, and have a realistic appraisal of your children's capacities of moral judgment. Only then should you make that trip to the cellphone store.

### Train your kids to make wise decisions.

Try as we might, we cannot shield our children from internet pornography or sexting completely. They will see it someday. When they do, if we have not also prepared them to process this moment in a healthy way, we will not have done everything within our power to minimize pornography's alluring power. Therefore, we must also begin training our children how to recognize and respond to porn.

Obviously, the place to begin is by talking with your children at an early age about what pornography is. One particularly helpful book for children is *Good Pictures Bad Pictures* by Kristen Jenson and Gail Poyner.[19] They encourage parents to have safe and natural conversations with their children about family pictures, identifying them as good. Then the parents let the children know that there are bad pictures too. These pictures show parts of the body we cover up when we go swimming. This is a simple and helpful way to begin these crucial conversations. The key is to keep the definition as clear and as accessible as possible—"Pornography is pictures or videos of people with few or no clothes on" or "Pornography usually shows videos of people having sex."[20]

Once you have a sense that your children can recognize pornography, you can equip them by giving them a plan for how to respond when they see it. The nonprofit Educate and Empower Kids offers a memorable acrostic that spells out how parents and kids can work together. It's called "Have a Plan to R-U-N." Here's how it works.[21]

### Recognize what you've seen and get away from it.

The goal is to help your kids name pornography when they see it. Remind them that nudity and obscene noises are helpful clues to remember. Then do some role playing that will allow them to practice what to say.

- Situation (kids): You're at a friend's house, and he or she wants to show you something on the computer. After a minute, you recognize that it is pornography. You might say, "This isn't cool; turn it off!" or "That's gross, and I don't want to see it."
- Situation (teens): You're with a friend, and he or she takes out a cell phone to show you something. It's porn. You could say, "You know that's not how sex really is, right?" or "Stuff like this is degrading to women *and* men."[22]

As you have more conversations, you will get a sense of what kinds of situations your children will be facing. If you can talk them through their response in advance, they will have a better chance to respond in a healthy way.

### Understand what you've seen and talk about how it made you feel with a trusted adult.

No matter the age when your child is confronted with porn, it will affect him in several ways. It will pique his curiosity, evoke shame, and even confuse him about the nature of sex. Talking with you or another safe and trustworthy adult about what he saw and how it made him feel without being condemned or shamed will keep the lines of communication open. These conversations shine the light on the secretive nature of porn, diminishing its power.

### Never seek it out again.

It will not take your kids long to figure out which friends are going to be pushing the porn agenda. Let them know that if they can't influence their friends not to watch it, then they should curtail their interactions with these friends or find new friends altogether.[23]

As you consider how you will utilize tools like the one above, remember that there is no silver bullet that will hit the target every time. In fact, your authentic and empathetic conversations may be some of the most influential and effective contributions you make to their future.

*Help your kids develop higher affections.*

We now turn to the ultimate antidote to the temptation of pornography—the power of a higher affection. Simply put, this means that pornography will lose its allure when our kids' hearts are filled with more positive devotions. As I observe friends who have struggled with porn, the driving force behind their newfound freedom is a deep realization that they in fact value some other things more than the temporary, visually induced feel-good drugs their bodies produce in their systems. They are committed to their marriages, to setting examples for their kids, and to maintaining pure hearts that allow them to see and experience God in a life-transforming way.

A stellar communicator from the previous century puts it well: "The safety of the Master in the presence of temptation lay in his complete and positive devotion to his mission: there was no unoccupied room in his soul where evil could find a home."[24] The take-home point for parents is that when we guide our children into positive, soul-filling experiences and commitments, porn is much less likely to get a hold on their heads and hearts.

A powerful example from Greek mythology illumines this truth. The Isle of Sirens was a dangerous temptation for sailors. The beautiful and enchanting music emanating from these erotic creatures lured many a sailor too close to the craggy shore. Before they could anchor safely, their vessels would be crushed by the rocks and waves, and they would lose their lives in pursuit of the promised pleasure. Two Greek heroes employed different strategies to navigate past the danger.

Ulysses had his crew tie him to the mast and fill his ears with wax so he couldn't hear the siren's song. His strategy was one of protection. If he could ensure that he would not hear their song and would be restrained from acting on what he was experiencing, he could survive.

And he did. It was effective, but it wasn't a very pleasant way to sail. In our context, if the only thing we do is put blinders over our kids' eyes and restrain them from any possibility of contact with the internet, we might save them from porn, but it will rob them of much of life.

Orpheus had a different approach. He sat on the deck with casual disinterest. Why? Because he was a musician too. He could make music more melodic and engaging than the sirens. Their music held no sway over him. Orpheus's strategy was one of preparation. He had practiced much and given his passion to a different song. So the Isle of Sirens lost its alluring power over him.

This, ultimately, is the mindset we want our children to have. Their world will be filled with more and more sexual imagery and innuendo. Protection will only get them so far. Eventually, they will have to have a more beautiful and compelling song in their heart than the siren song of pornography if they are going to navigate these dangerous waters successfully.

So how do you help your children write this kind of music in their lives? The place to begin is to help them discover and develop three passions. The first passion is simply what they are interested in and wired to do. Whether it's the arts, athletics, academics, computers, or gaming, come alongside them with encouragement and support so they can grow and excel in an area that is important to them. When they work and practice hard and then succeed, they are creating a strong reward circuit in their brains that will make getting caught up in porn less likely. Their stronger devotion to this endeavor will reduce the time, energy, and emotional bandwidth available for porn to hijack.

Second, helping them develop a passion for God will be indispensable in preparing them to navigate the treacherous waters of pornography. Begin by modeling a life guided and shaped by your own spiritual sense of calling and passion. If they see you living out your life and following Jesus with passion and vulnerability, they will be drawn to the God who is transforming you. As their parents, you will have the single best opportunity to shape and form their understanding of who God is, and that will create the framework on which they will build their faith and life.

In this same regard, the church you choose to attend as a family can have a significant impact on your children's preparedness to face the temptation of pornography. Look for two qualities in a youth group that will support your efforts in their lives. Seek out a student ministry that understands the porn crisis we are facing and sets appropriate boundaries in its ministry that reinforce your efforts to protect your kids from interaction with pornography. Couple this with a student ministry whose view of God is most clearly revealed in the character of Jesus—full of grace and mercy, not judgment and condemnation. When you find these two criteria at work, you will soon notice your children's hearts are full of God's love and presence, and they will want to experience it more and more. It will become a powerful higher affection.

There is one last passion to help your child develop, and that is the passion to serve others. I believe C.S. Lewis was correct when he wrote, "The danger of pornography is of coming to love the prison of self."[25] On most occasions, indulging in porn is an intensely self-focused activity. Lewis reminds us that it requires nothing of us and promises only benefits for us. If you want to prepare the heart of your child to resist pornography, involve her in experiences that lead her away from herself and broaden her perspectives of the world.

As early as you deem appropriate, take your children with you to feed the homeless. If you can, take them on a mission trip to an orphanage in a third-world country and let them see the hurt and brokenness of the world and experience the joy of meeting Jesus in the lives of the people they love and serve. Jesus meant it when he said it is more blessed to give than to receive. When older children and teens get a taste of the presence of God in this way, they can develop a holy passion that seals out the siren call of the flesh that would impair their judgment and lead them down a path of disappointment and disillusionment.

## Concluding Thoughts

As I rehearse the active verbs I have been encouraging you to exercise—protect and prepare—it dawns on me again that we are talking about a process and a journey. It is not a single conversation with your kids. It is multiple conversations. It is not about getting the next big universal security software program for all their devices so you can sit back in faux security. Rather, it's about faithful diligence to stay ahead of the game so you can continue to protect them from themselves and others. It's not about shaming and judging them so harshly that they stay away from porn because of guilt and fear. It's about calling them to the passionate life God has in mind for them while reminding them that looking at porn is like reaching for cotton candy when a steak dinner is set before them. In a real sense, we are fighting for the souls of our children. It will not be easy or comfortable, but it will be worth it. The stakes are far too high and the regrets far too long lasting if we don't.

......................................................................................

*Dear Lord,*

*As I think about the world my children are growing up in, my mind and heart easily become paralyzed by fear. The abuse and misuse of the gift of sex is rampant. Its counterfeits pervade almost every visual space. How, O Lord, can I protect and prepare them to know and love others as you so graciously intend? I am depending on you for wisdom, grace, and courage. Help me think clearly about the right boundaries. Give me strength to make the hard choices necessary for their growth and wholeness. And keep my heart pure.*

*Amen.*

## Breaking It Down for Every Age

Pervasive, hard-core pornography has become an inescapable reality of our internet age. The World Wide Web is an untamed Wild West of illicit content, and it goes without saying that as parents we must be diligent to protect our kids online. However, we must also acknowledge that it is impossible to completely shield our kids from porn. Therefore, our willingness to talk to them about it at every developmental stage can have a far-reaching impact on their emotional and relational health.

### Elementary-Aged Kids

Even at this young age, it is crucial that kids are equipped with an understanding of what pornography is and a strategy for how to respond when they encounter it. Talk to your child about both of these, as outlined in this chapter. Proactively addressing this topic will go a long way toward removing the shame and confusion that would prompt your child to keep a brush with pornography secret from you. Even if you decide not to give your child a smartphone or internet-enabled tablet during his elementary school years, many of his friends will likely have this technology. As discussed in this chapter, prepare your child with a response should his friends show him pornography on their devices. Talk through various scenarios and possible responses, and check in with your child regularly about how his friends are navigating technology, what apps he's using, and what he's encountering online.

### Tweens

During these preteen years, your child's online presence will likely increase as social media gains prominence in her life and friendships. Make careful, educated decisions about social media with your tween, and go before her onto social platforms so you're more aware of what those environments hold. Set boundaries around the hours your tween has access to her device, and talk frankly with her about sexting. Remember also that helping your tween develop some healthy passions as addressed in this chapter can go a long way toward guiding her heart and mind toward soul-filling pastimes that crowd out the clamor of porn.

## Teens

As online freedoms increase for your teen, help him understand the role of accountability in healthy relationships. Talk to your teen about how healthy adult relationships thrive on integrity and accountability and about the relational damage that can come from isolation and secrecy. If safeguards are built in to your own online interactions, share those with your teen, and tell him how you are accountable to the important people in your life for what you view online, whether your spouse, your employer, or your close friends. Help your teen build accountability into his online interactions, with the understanding that it is a vital building block to successful adult relationships. If you sense that your teen might be struggling with porn or questions about it that he isn't willing to discuss with you, encourage him to talk to a trusted youth pastor or other adult who can offer guidance in this area.

## Questions for Personal Reflection or Group Discussion

1. Think back to your first experience seeing porn. What feelings and thoughts did that experience evoke?
2. As you reflect on this chapter, what concerns you most about your children and the pervasiveness and accessibility of pornography?
3. We have dual roles as parents—to protect our children and to prepare them. How are you currently protecting your children from porn? What do you need to do next?

4. How are you preparing your children to say no to porn when you are not around? What do you need to do next in this regard?
5. How can you cultivate "higher affections" in your children's hearts so that the allure of pornography is diminished?

## Additional Resources

If you are interested in further reading on this subject, these resources may be helpful.

### For Parents

*How to Talk to Your Kids About Pornography* by Educate and Empower Kids

*Wired for Intimacy: How Pornography Hijacks the Male Brain* by William Struthers

*Your Brain on Porn* by Gary Wilson

### For Children

*Good Pictures Bad Pictures: Porn-Proofing Today's Young Kids* by Kristen Jenson and Gail Poyner

*The Talk: 7 Lessons to Introduce Your Child to Biblical Sexuality* by Luke Gilkerson

# Same-Sex Attraction

## Paul Basden

Had we written this book a dozen years ago, I am not sure we would have included a chapter on same-sex attraction. The topic of homosexuality was certainly being discussed and debated nationwide at that time and was gaining momentum in social awareness. For example…

- Ellen DeGeneres appeared on the cover of *Time* magazine in 1997 alongside the title "Yep, I'm Gay."

- Several million people from the LGBTQ community joined in gay rights parades throughout the 1990s in cities such as Atlanta, Boston, New York City, and San Francisco. Political dignitaries raised the parade profiles by participating in the events—including Mayor Rudolph Giuliani and Senate candidate Hillary Rodham Clinton, who in June 2000 proudly marched down Fifth Avenue in New York's Gay Day Parade.[1]

- Gene Robinson, Episcopal bishop of New Hampshire, was ordained to the priesthood in 2003, the first openly gay priest in the Anglican Church to attain that status. The vote was divided then, and the aftershocks are still being felt in the Anglican Communion.

But things have changed in American culture over the last decade at what seems like warp speed.

- Katy Perry released a hit single in 2008 titled "I Kissed a Girl," which went to the top of the charts immediately and stayed there for seven weeks, selling more than four and a half million digital copies.
- The musical comedy-drama series *Glee* launched on the Fox Television Network in 2009 and featured multiple episodes in which high school characters explored their sexual orientations and identities. The show was wildly popular in America, garnering multiple Emmy Awards and high Nielsen ratings.
- The Supreme Court of the United States ruled in 2015 that same-sex marriages are legal nationwide, touching off celebration in the LGBTQ community and creating angst for marriage traditionalists.

Our culture has felt a tectonic shift in recent years regarding same-sex issues. A topic that you likely would never have talked to your parents about a generation ago is a question that is absolutely on your children's minds today.

In the current conversation, several words are used in related or interchangeable ways, including "homosexual," "lesbian," "gay," and "same-sex orientation" (or "attraction"). In this chapter, I will primarily, but not exclusively, use the phrase "same-sex." That means the question before us is, what do we tell our kids about same-sex attraction? The goal of this chapter is to bring more light than heat to the discussion as we explore the topic through the lens of God's written Word, the Bible, and God's living Word, Jesus Christ.

We will explore this question in three ways:

- What does the Bible teach about same-sex attraction and behavior?[2]
- What does the Bible teach about loving your neighbor?

- What topics are your children likely to bring up that the Bible doesn't address but that you will need to help them think through as a Christ-follower?

## A Gift for a Male-Female Relationship

The place to start in Scripture is not with passages about same-sex couples, but with the primary passage on sex and sexuality—the creation account. Why? Because the Bible speaks about sex before it speaks about same-sex issues. "So God created mankind in his own image, in the image of God he created him; male and female he created them. God blessed them and said to them, 'Be fruitful and increase in number; fill the earth and subdue it'" (Genesis 1:27-28).

Here we find a universal biblical principle: God created humans in two different but complementary genders and commanded them to continue their existence through propagation. The male-female distinction is fixed in the creation story. Gender and sexuality are introduced in the earliest chapters of the Bible as a pattern of creation designed by God.[3] Simply said, in the beginning, God intended opposites to attract.

With this pattern in mind, let's look at the primary biblical references to homosexuality—two in the Old Testament and two in the New Testament.[4]

When we start with the Old Testament law, we find two specific teachings in Leviticus. Chapter 18 lists a host of sexual practices that the Israelites were to avoid because they offended God. Such practices would have been familiar to the people of God because they were practiced in Egypt (their old home) and Canaan (their new home). Here's the prologue to this list of sexual sins:

> You must not do as they do in Egypt, where you used to live, and you must not do as they do in the land of Canaan, where I am bringing you. Do not follow their practices.

You must obey my laws and be careful to follow my decrees. I am the LORD your God (Leviticus 18:3-4).

The God of Israel, who was different from all other gods, wanted his covenant people to be different from all other peoples, so he gave them unambiguous commands—including sanctions about sex. Through these laws he established clear boundaries for his people. There could be no sexual relations with family members (acts of incest), with someone else's spouse (acts of adultery), with someone of the same gender (acts of homosexuality), or with animals (acts of bestiality). All these practices ignored God's permissible sexual boundaries—sexual intimacy between a husband and a wife. Every other sexual expression was out of bounds. In this context, we read a specific injunction in Leviticus 18:22: "Do not have sexual relations with a man as one does with a woman; that is detestable."

Leviticus 20 lists the sins that merited the death penalty in ancient Israel: child sacrifice, cursing one's parents, adultery, incest, homosexuality, bestiality, and so on. The same-sex taboo is repeated in Leviticus 20:13: "If a man has sexual relations with a man as one does with a woman, both of them have done what is detestable."

Obviously, we don't put people to death today for any of these practices. And I for one am grateful—I might have been arrested and killed at the age of 12 for the way I disrespected my parents! Today we reserve capital punishment for capital crimes. But these practices were so offensive and morally out of bounds to God's covenant people, he set up the death penalty as a deterrent.

This raises a crucial question your older children may ask: Does the Old Testament law still apply to us today?

Some people argue that the Old Testament Jewish law has no authority over New Testament Christians. Certainly that's true on some issues. We don't keep the kosher dietary laws, the ritual ceremonial laws, or the blood sacrifices that were mandated back then. Why? Because we find in the New Testament that either Jesus or his followers repudiated those laws. We are no longer bound by them. Yet we must not forget that what the New Testament affirms from the Old Testament still applies to Christ-followers.

When you come to the New Testament, you discover that the apostle Paul addressed homosexuality three times. The two most important passages are found in Romans and 1 Corinthians.

Romans 1 opens with an affirmation of the good news of salvation. It concludes with Paul's explanation as to why the news is so good: All people are sinful before God—no exceptions. It doesn't matter if you are Jew or Gentile, if you are familiar with or ignorant of the law. Everyone knows enough about God to worship him, but instead we have worshipped idols and images. Because of our rebellion, evidenced in our decision to reject God and live in spiritual and moral darkness, God has allowed us to experience the full consequences of our sins. When Paul lists the sins and consequences of this pattern of rebellion, the first example he gives is homosexual behavior, which was common in the Greco-Roman world of the first century and would be well known to his readers. Here is what he wrote.

> Because of this, God gave them over to shameful lusts. Even their women exchanged natural sexual relations for unnatural ones. In the same way the men also abandoned natural relations with women and were inflamed with lust for one another. Men committed shameful acts with other men, and received in themselves the due penalty for their error (Romans 1:26-27).

A straightforward reading of the text shows that when people rejected God's natural order and pattern of sex between male and female and crossed the divinely appointed boundary line into homosexual behavior, God judged them. That much seems clear.

But the passage does not stop there. Paul has just gotten started. He then lists other examples of human revolt against God that led to divine judgment—yet none of the vices are sexual.

They have become filled with every kind of wickedness, evil, greed and depravity. They are full of envy, murder, strife, deceit and malice. They are gossips, slanderers, God-haters, insolent, arrogant and boastful; they invent ways of doing evil; they disobey their parents; they have no understanding, no fidelity, no love, no mercy (Romans 1:29-31).

In God's eyes, these attitudes and actions are all sins. It's easy to say God is opposed to same-sex relationships, but it's just as true that God is opposed to gossip, pride, and envy. I've never engaged in any type of same-sex behavior, but I have surely earned multiple gold medals in gossip, pride, and envy.

The point is, homosexual acts are considered sinful in this passage, but so is everything else on the list. Singling out and holding up homosexual behavior above everything else on the list is bad Bible application.

Next we turn to 1 Corinthians 6, where we find several paragraphs dedicated to sex. What was going on in Corinth that called for this apostolic confrontation? Evidently, sex in Corinth was hot and heavy, seedy and steamy, and available around the clock—especially in pagan temples, where prostitution was the norm. The culture in that day was as sexualized as ours is today, maybe even more so. In fact, some scholars believe that "Corinthianize" was a euphemism for having sex.

Because Corinth was a popular and prominent port city, Paul planted a church there. Most who confessed faith in Jesus Christ entered the church as typical Corinthians—sexually promiscuous. Because of their cultural background, Paul told them to avoid sexual sin at all costs.

Do you not know that wrongdoers will not inherit the kingdom of God? Do not be deceived: Neither the sexually immoral nor idolaters nor adulterers nor men who have sex with men nor thieves nor the greedy nor drunkards nor

slanderers nor swindlers will inherit the kingdom of God
(1 Corinthians 6:9-10).

Just as Moses told the Old Testament people to be different from
the culture surrounding them, so Paul says the same thing to the New
Testament people. He names similar vices to avoid: engaging in premarital sex, adultery, and homosexual acts. But again he doesn't stop
there. He goes on to identify nonsexual offenders, such as thieves,
greedy people, and drunkards. Again, you may think you are off the
hook if you are not practicing same-sex behavior. But do you struggle with stealing? Greed? Alcohol? These sins are found in the same
"do not" list.

The highlight of the passage is in verse 11, where Paul exclaims,
"That is what some of you were. But you were washed, you were sanc-
tified, you were justified in the name of the Lord Jesus Christ and by
the Spirit of our God."

In other words, "Some of you used to live just like that. But in
Jesus Christ and through the Holy Spirit, you are a different person!
Now live differently!"

In these two passages, Paul clearly affirmed the Old Testament
prohibition against homosexual behavior. He echoed the perspective that it was sinful and morally out of bounds. But interestingly,
he never treated it as the most egregious iniquity or the one sin God
won't forgive. In fact, he always included it along with other sins of
the body, sins of the mouth, and sins of the heart. His point is, it's a
sin—one of many.

Let's summarize. On the one hand, we can affirm the Bible's
teachings on same-sex behavior and believe that to disregard them is a
mistake. Ethicist Tony Campolo spoke for many of us years ago when
he affirmed, "Our obedience to the teachings of the Bible necessitates
that we withhold approval of homosexual intercourse."[5]

On the other hand, we have no biblical warrant to make a homosexual act the "*Scarlet Letter* sin" that is worse than all other sins,

especially all sexual sins. According to these four Bible passages, heterosexual sin is clearly just as sinful as homosexual sin. God does not approve of adultery, fornication (which includes premarital sex), or addiction to pornography. One must ignore a simple and plain reading of the Bible to reach any other conclusion.

Perhaps you are asking, what about Jesus? Did he ever speak about same-sex relationships or homosexual behavior? Good question. And the answer is…Jesus was silent about it. We may interpret his silence as an indicator of tacit approval, but I believe it makes more sense to regard it as evidence that Jesus, as a first-century Jew, felt no need to comment on something the law said was morally out of bounds. If you choose the former interpretation, you are left to conclude that Jesus and Paul are in conflict on this issue, and you must choose between them. But there is no need to get stuck on the horns of this dilemma. Jesus and Paul were faithful Jews who held to the ethical teachings of the Torah, so they would have understood sexual morality in the same way.

However, let's not write off Jesus too quickly.

## God Intends Us to Love Others. Period.

Though Jesus has nothing to say about same-sex issues, he does weigh in very decidedly about a related matter—how we are to treat our neighbor. Jesus is unambiguous about our duty to love others. When asked to name the greatest commandment in Scripture, Jesus had to give two: Love God fully, and love your neighbor as yourself (Matthew 22:39).

In Luke's account of this exchange, when Jesus was asked, "Who is my neighbor?" he told the story of the good Samaritan. If we were to contemporize this story, we could substitute for the Samaritan anyone who is identified with a group in society that is despised and shunned. And if this parable teaches anything, it teaches that your neighbor, whom you are to love, is anyone in need. Given how often homosexuals are resented, reviled, and rejected in our society, they clearly need love. When it comes to anyone with same-sex attraction, Christians are called to love them sacrificially, with compassion and kindness, as we love ourselves. This does not require approval of their lifestyle or choices. But if you are a Christ-follower, Jesus calls you to love them in word and deed. No exceptions allowed.

We need to say one more thing about Jesus: He was always reaching out to outcasts, whether they were lepers, prostitutes, tax collectors, or adulterers. If you and I are following Jesus, we will reach out to those who are treated like outcasts in our society—and people with same-sex attraction often fall into that camp.

Jesus says, "Love your neighbor as yourself," not "Love your neighbor if you agree with their sexual behavior or their political affiliation or their religious views." Simply "love your neighbor."

In summary, the Bible is clear about two things: Homosexuality is outside God's pattern of sexual relations inasmuch as the Bible never affirms it, and we are to love our neighbor, whether homosexual or heterosexual, in the same way that we love ourselves.

## The Need for Wisdom

The Bible doesn't answer every question on this issue, but godly wisdom helps us find helpful insights. Here are five often-asked questions that Scripture doesn't address that call for candid conversations and discerning responses.

### 1. Why are some people homosexual? Do they choose it, or is it chosen for them? Is it nature or nurture?

I am neither a physician nor a psychologist or sociologist. But over the years, I have visited with several people who are or have been in same-sex relationships. They've told me different stories.

One gay friend of mine grew up in a strong Christian home, dated girls in high school and college, got engaged to the girl of his dreams, eventually broke off the engagement, struggled with the awareness that he was not heterosexual, eventually met another gay man, and then made a lifelong commitment to him. They have been faithful to each other for 30 years. Today this gentleman is a grace-filled Christ-follower who still struggles with his sexual orientation. He told me, "I may never understand myself." Contrary to popular assumptions, he experienced no sexual abuse growing up—no evil uncle, no passive father or overpowering mother. He simply knew by his teenage years that he was homosexual. He would say he has always been attracted to males rather than females.

Another gay friend knew he was not heterosexual by the time he entered high school, but he felt it was socially necessary to ignore it rather than admit it. He got married, had a child, and then got divorced. Along the way, he felt God call him into ministry, so he went to seminary and began serving churches. Faced with single-ness as an adult and the awareness that he was homosexual, he chose to remain sexually abstinent for the next ten years. He decided to explore the gay lifestyle for a brief period in his midforties, but after much prayer and soul-searching, he eventually chose abstinence as a way of life. He then sought ordination in another church tradition and again effectively served as a minister for several years.

Eventually he came to a turning point. He concluded that the only way to be true to himself was to accept his sexual orientation. Today he is a grace-filled, loving pastor of a church that fully embraces same-sex relationships. Like the first story, this one does not include any sexual abuse, an evil uncle, a passive father, or an overpowering mother in his childhood. Yet my friend knew he was not heterosex-ual by the time he reached puberty. For him, this is not a choice—it's a given.

I also know of two other men who struggle with being gay. Tragi-cally, both were sexually abused as children—one by an older boy in the neighborhood, the other by a family member. Without a doubt, these events have colored their sexual identity and choices ever since. It's not clear to either of them whether their homosexuality is from nature or nurture.

A female friend of mine grew up in a home where all the family dynamics worked against her developing a healthy sexuality. She had a mother who was manipulative, deceptive, and adulterous—not to mention physically, verbally, and emotionally abusive. She had a passive father. She was raped at the age of 14 by an uncle and experienced several failed dating relationships with guys during her teen years.

Amid that confusion and pain she cried out, "I'm done with men! I wonder if women are any better." In her late teens and early twenties, she explored lesbianism with a few close girlfriends for a time but found it unfulfilling. She concluded, "I guess women are no better than men." She told me she was just looking for love in all the wrong places. Now she believes that her lesbian experimentation was situational, not biological.

We may never know with certainty the answer to this question, but we can ponder what one Christian sociologist has observed: "Most male homosexuals did not consciously choose their orientation," whereas most lesbians have chosen that lifestyle because of sociological and/or psychological causes. But nobody knows for sure.[6]

## 2. Why do some teens experiment with a gay lifestyle?

Adolescence is the time when teens discover their sexuality—its identity, drive, and power. Most teens move somewhat easily through this phase into healthy heterosexuality. Some adolescents, however, remain unclear about their sexual identity. They may experiment with same-sex relationships, which can be especially attractive if people whom they respect are going down that same road—whether a teacher, a coach, or a team captain. After such experimentation, many (but not all) teens reverse direction and embrace heterosexuality.

We can't identify every reason a young person may take this route, but we would be naive to underestimate the power of pop culture on teens' views and values. When Madonna can kiss Britney Spears on the mouth and Sandra Bullock can kiss Meryl Streep on the mouth in front of millions of TV viewers and to the delight of all Hollywood, then lesbianism has become cool to untold numbers of girls and young women. So, Mom and Dad, watch what your kids are watching, talk with them about it, and help them navigate wisely the sexual discoveries of adolescence.

### 3. Is there a difference between same-sex attraction and same-sex behavior?

If a person is biologically homosexual (whether through hormone imbalance or genetic ordering or any other explanation), then God condemns neither that disposition nor that person. Why? Because God condemns actions, not dispositions. All of us have certain inborn traits that we would love to get rid of with a magic wand. It may be a hot temper that alienates loved ones, insecurity and fear that lead to anxiety, or a chemical addiction that ruins relationships. God doesn't judge our disposition—he judges our actions. That is, he doesn't judge your alcoholic tendencies, but your alcoholic consumption. He doesn't judge your inclination to anger, but your outbursts of temper. He doesn't judge your same-sex tendency, but your same-sex behavior.

Same-sex attraction is clearly different from same-sex behavior.

### 4. Can a homosexual become a heterosexual?

I have no firsthand knowledge by which to answer this question. But here is what I believe from reading books and articles and from talking with people: Some gays have tried to change their sexual preferences and succeeded, and their stories are courageous and inspirational. Many others have prayed and sought change but to no avail. In *What's So Amazing About Grace?*, Philip Yancey recounts the story of his good friend Mel White, who in the 1980s was a married father of two with a successful career as a Christian author and speaker.

After struggling for years with his sexual identity, in his midforties Mel admitted to his wife that he was gay. He also told her he wanted to get rid of his homosexual feelings through whatever means were at his disposal. He went to a counselor for psychological therapy, he took medications for hormonal therapy, he had Christian leaders anoint him with oil and pray for him to be healed. He even tried exorcism in case he was dealing with demon possession. When none of those approaches worked, Mel tried suicide. Thankfully he was unsuccessful. Today he is living with his same-sex partner and still considers Philip Yancey as a valued and trusted friend.[7]

More recently, Andrew Marin tells the story of John, who at the age of 15 came to realize he was different from all the other boys he knew. With that realization, he slowly and sadly began to shut himself off from others, afraid they might suspect what he was hoping to hide. John grew up in a home with parents, brothers, and sisters who were Christians. He went to a Christian high school and later attended a large evangelical college, where he was elected student body president. But at 15, John was mostly scared. He determined he would pray a prayer every night until it was answered: "Lord, when I wake up in the morning, please just let me be straight like everyone else." That prayer flowed from his heart every night for the next 15 years. "And every morning for fifteen years he woke up dejected and broken because he still had the same attractions he never wanted in the first place." By his midthirties, John reached two possible conclusions about God: Either there was no God, because his prayers were never answered, or God wasn't answering those prayers because he had already condemned him to hell because of his same-sex feelings.[8]

John Burke, pastor of Gateway Community Church in Austin, Texas, where many gays attend and actively participate, says that while some gays he knows have successfully changed their sexual orientations, they are in the minority. He counsels, "We must live within the tension of loving and accepting gay people seeking to follow Christ, recognizing that their orientation may never change."[9]

### 5. How should the church respond to people engaged in same-sex relationships?

My friend Fisher Humphreys has helped me see that churches tend to respond to this issue in multiple ways. I have taken the liberty of abbreviating his six approaches to three.[10]

The first is rejection. Churches that take this approach are marked by hatred, disgust, and fear of homosexuals. Their message is, "Stay away from us." Their attitude is symbolized by a closed fist, suggesting not just rejection, but militancy.

The second is championing. Churches that champion homosexuality fully approve of homosexual behavior as an alternative lifestyle, equivalent in purpose and value to heterosexual marriage. Their message is, "We celebrate your same-sex orientation, relationships, and decisions. More than that, we celebrate gay marriage. We even celebrate the ordination of gay ministers." The symbol of their attitude is a high five—"We won!"

A third approach is welcoming. Churches that adopt this attitude are marked by acceptance of homosexuals as persons of worth and value made in the image of God but not of homosexuality as a lifestyle. They accept same-sex orientations without accepting same-sex behavior. The message they hope to send is, "We value you and care for you even if we don't agree with your decisions." The symbol of this approach is a handshake—which for all of us, in any setting, points to a grace-filled welcome, even without an agreement of principles.[11]

## Conclusion

I can't predict where this subject personally intersects your life. You may have a family member, friend, or coworker who is gay. You may have struggled with issues of sexual identity yourself. You may have a child who is confused about his or her sexual orientation. All of us can relate to this topic in some way, so let me offer some humble suggestions for guiding your children as they relate to people with same-sex attraction.

**Question:** What do you say to someone who is attracted to or involved with someone of the same sex?

**Answer:** You are valuable to God. While I cannot agree with your lifestyle, I value you as a human made in the image of God. I feel awkward in knowing how to respond to you, but I won't let that stop me from caring about you. If you are a Christ-follower, I accept you as my brother or sister in Christ, even if I do not support your lifestyle choice. Forgive me for all the times I have ignored or excluded you. I simply want to follow Jesus's teaching to love you.

**Question:** What do you say to someone who is heterosexual but is harsh in his or her treatment of same-sex individuals or couples?

**Answer:** If your primary reaction toward homosexuals is hatred or fear and you know that is not God's will, ask God to change your heart. Seek to understand people who are living with a condition they may not have chosen. We are all equal at the foot of the cross—there is no room for condemnation there. Intentionally welcome gay persons and get to know them at church, at work, and in your neighborhood. There's a ton of truth in the statement "Once you know someone's story, you can't hate them any longer."

How to respond to individuals with a same-sex orientation is still a polarizing issue in our world. But as Christ-followers, we must learn to live within the tension of following the biblical teaching that same-sex behavior is morally out of bounds for God's people yet expressing God's love and Jesus's compassion to all people, gay and straight. It's a real tension, and it makes us feel uncomfortable. But it is our calling and our privilege if we intend to follow Jesus as Lord. After all, he believed greed was out of bounds and yet loved Zacchaeus. He believed adultery was out of bounds and yet loved the Samaritan woman. He believed cowardice was out of bounds and yet loved Simon Peter. This is the heart of Jesus! Help your child see it…in you.

*O Lord,*

*I need a double dose of your wisdom to talk to my children about this topic. It's so controversial that there seems to be little room for healthy conversation. But that's what I'm asking for—wisdom. Please open the doors for me to talk to my kids about same-sex orientation and behavior. When we talk, help me listen to what they're thinking and feeling. And when I open my mouth, let your wisdom flow.*

*To be honest, I'm afraid they're more knowledgeable of the subject than I am! I don't want to look like a dinosaur in what I say, but I also know my kids need to be led spiritually. If I avoid this topic because I'm scared, I will forfeit my chance to influence my children. So give me courage along with wisdom.*

*If you give me those two gifts in abundance, I think I can make it. Thank you in advance.*

*Amen.*

## Breaking It Down for Every Age

Same-sex attraction can be a deeply divisive and emotionally charged topic with which thoughtful, Bible-believing adults grapple. You may have friends or relatives living a gay lifestyle, which means questions about homosexuality hit particularly close to home for your family. Below are some suggestions for answering your kids' questions about this weighty topic in a helpful, age-appropriate manner. For all these conversations, at every stage, the foundation must be love—God's love for all people and his clear call for us to love them too.

### Elementary-Aged Kids

Some of the earliest questions kids ask about same-sex relationships may arise because of depictions they see in popular culture.

Increasingly, "family" TV shows, movies, and books include same-sex characters and story lines. Their questions also may be prompted by someone in their life—a schoolmate, neighbor, or family member—who has same-sex parents. Perhaps the most effective instruction you will give your kids at this stage will be your own behavior toward people in same-sex relationships. Model an unthreatened and genuinely welcoming posture for your children, and remember that kids at this stage tend to think in very black-and-white terms. It may stretch them (as it stretches you) to help them comprehend that while God does not approve of certain choices people make, his love for them is not diminished by those choices. Help your children understand that our primary responsibility as followers of Jesus is to show love to all people, even those with whom we disagree.

## Tweens

During the tween years, your children may begin to question the biblical boundaries related to sexuality. As they grapple with a biblical viewpoint that prohibits behavior they see celebrated throughout popular culture, they may ask uncomfortable questions. They may make comments that run counter to the values you want to promote. Encourage your tweens to voice their questions, and as you engage in these conversations, remember your goal is not to defend a position or win an argument. Your goal is to point your tweens toward life-long relationships with Jesus.

## Teens

As your child enters the teen years, the issue of same-sex attraction will probably become more personal as some of his peers come out as gay. Be prepared to help your teen process these revelations from a position of love and grace. As you talk to your teen about same-sex issues, be honest when you don't have easy answers. Be willing to live within the tension stated in this chapter—following the biblical teaching that same-sex behavior is morally out of bounds for God's people yet expressing God's love and Jesus's compassion to all people, gay and straight.

## Questions for Personal Reflection or Group Discussion

1. How old do you think your child should be for you to bring up the idea that sex is God's gift?
2. Has your child talked to you about same-sex relationships? What led to the conversation—a movie or TV show? School or neighborhood talk? A friend or family member?
3. What scares you about talking to your child about male-female attraction versus same-sex attraction?
4. If you have a coworker, neighbor, or friend who is gay or lesbian, have you shown them the love of Christ? When you do, what do you think your child is learning?

## Additional Resources

If you are interested in further reading on this subject, these resources may be helpful.

### For Parents

*Love Is an Orientation* by Andrew Marin

*Messy Grace* by Caleb Kaltenbach

*Single, Gay, Christian* by Gregory Coles

*Slaves, Women, and Homosexuals* by William J. Webb

*Welcoming but Not Affirming* by Stanley J. Grenz

## 10

# Drugs and Alcohol

### Jim Johnson

The quiet routine of my Wednesday evening was interrupted by a phone call from a longtime friend. Charlie's voice was heavy and breaking with emotion as he delivered the dreadful news. His 27-year-old son, Walton, was on life support in a West Texas hospital and not expected to live. Charlie was so anguished, I picked up the word "overdose" but not much more. Charlie and his wife, Becky, were on a five-hour drive to an uncertain future in a strange town where they knew no one. He asked me if I would pray for them.

"Of course," I said. "Let me throw some things in the car, and I'll meet you there."

I rendezvoused with another close friend on the way, and we arrived deep in a September night to find Becky and Charlie coping one moment and then reeling the next at what they were facing. Walton was indeed on life support and had no discernible brain function. The only hope the doctors offered was "We'll have to wait and see."

The next three days were filled with intermittent waves of weeping, waiting, praying, and hoping. Then, thanks be to God and the gifted healers in the intensive care unit, Walton came out of his coma. All the worries and fears of lasting impairments soon came to naught, and within a month Walton was released from the hospital. Vocational and drug rehab were ordered, and three months after the overdose, Walton moved back to Midland, Texas, to continue his work. To those of us on the outside looking in, there was great hope that Walton's story was going to be rewritten with a much more hopeful trajectory.

That was not to be the case, however. On January 30, 2015, less than a month after returning to work, Walton died of an overdose alone in his apartment in Midland. Since that time, I have watched with deep reverence how Becky and Charlie, in separate ways, have grieved and grown through this unspeakable loss. As I pondered how I would begin this chapter, I decided to ask them if I could share Walton's story. Both agreed without hesitation, voicing a hope that a part of God's redemption of Walton's loss would be that others might heed their cautionary tale and be spared the same crushing conclusion.

Walton, when he was 14, started commenting that he thought smoking pot was okay. Becky, a bit concerned, began giving him research on the impact of marijuana use. Nothing came from the exchange, but soon Becky and Charlie began noticing that some of the painkillers prescribed for family members following recent surgeries were missing. They confronted Walton with their suspicions, and he admitted to taking the meds for recreational use. He assured them that he was very self-aware and was in no danger of becoming addicted to them. Becky and Charlie were not convinced, and their apprehension began to spike.

As it turned out, Walton was not that self-aware, and his drug use began to spin out of control. Even though he would graduate from college and finish law school, his recurring episodes of disconnection, dishonesty, and confusion were increasingly incapacitating for Walton and worrisome for Charlie and Becky. So it was devastating but not surprising when they got the first call telling them that Walton had overdosed. What *was* surprising, though, was how quickly he returned to taking drugs after rehab—even before he arrived back in Midland. When Becky realized this, she knew in her heart that "this story wasn't going to have a good ending."

When I asked Becky if she would share with me how she has emotionally processed Walton's story, she had some vulnerable, raw, and honest reflections. I think they are especially instructive as we begin this chapter.

> There are so many mixed emotions. On one hand, I felt like I had done everything I could to help Walton, but on the other hand, I wish I would have done more. What if I had confronted his drug use earlier when I thought he was smoking pot? Could I have nipped it in the bud? Were the marital problems that Charlie and I had a cause of Walton's drug use? What if I had insisted on sending him to rehab? At the time, I thought that rehab wouldn't work unless he wanted it, but should I have tried?

With these thoughts, Becky is inviting us into her personal postmortem. She is asking the hard questions, wondering what, if anything, she could have done to change the plotline of Walton's story. This process is incredibly painful for anyone and is exacerbated by the fact that no one will know the answers to these questions this side of heaven. I'm so grateful Becky was willing to share her experience with us.

That is why I am so intent on leveraging her story for your benefit as a parent who may one day be facing these very issues. Here's how I hope to do it. If Becky could have known then what she knows now, she might have had a much better chance of changing the outcome. Considering this, I am going to challenge you in this chapter to do a parental "premortem." A premortem is projecting yourself into an undesired future and then looking back to determine what must be done to avoid that outcome. No caring and thoughtful parent plans for their children to fall victim to drug or alcohol addiction, but the terrible truth is that very few parents intentionally plan for their kids *not* to. Why is this? Because when it comes to the issues of alcohol and drugs, parenting is tough stuff!

## Present Problems

Interactions with our children do not take place in a vacuum. Genetic wiring, family dynamics, and present realities all play into the how, what, and when of these crucial conversations. I cannot speak to the first two factors in your case, but I can offer some thoughts on the broader context in which we seek to guide and prepare our children. Currently, three substance abuse trends are dominating news cycles and impacting the well-being of individuals, families, institutions, and entire communities. Each one of these developments is causing parents, educators, church leaders, business leaders, politicians, and law enforcement agencies to rethink and recalibrate how they are going to respond to these real threats to our common good.

### Alcohol Abuse and Binge Drinking

According to the CDC, "Binge drinking is the most common, costly, and deadly pattern of excessive alcohol use in the United States, especially among individuals between the ages of 18 and 34."[1] In a recent national survey, almost 60 percent of college students between the ages of 18 and 22 drank alcohol in the previous month,[2] and almost two-thirds of them engaged in binge drinking during that time.[3] Binge drinking is defined as men consuming five or more drinks or women consuming four or more drinks in a two-hour period.[4]

The consequences of alcohol abuse among college students are staggering. Researchers now estimate that 1,825 students 18 to 24 will lose their lives in alcohol-related accidents each year. Nearly 700,000 will be assaulted by another student who has been drinking, and 97,000 will experience alcohol-related sexual assault or date rape. Twenty percent of students meet the criteria for alcohol abuse disorder, and 25 percent report academic consequences, such as missing class, doing poorly on exams or papers, and receiving lower grades, due to their alcohol use.[5]

## The Opioid Epidemic

The proliferation of opioid-based painkillers began in the 1990s when pharmaceutical companies assured the medical community that patients would not become addicted to these drugs. As a result, more and more physicians prescribed them and at higher rates. The outcome of this tragic misjudgment is a medical crisis.[6]

The number of individuals who are addicted to and dying from opioids is astounding. An estimated 2.4 million Americans are addicted to prescription pain medications, such as Vicodin and Percocet. These numbers don't include those who are addicted to heroin and other illegal drugs. In 2016, 64,000 Americans died from opioids and other drugs.[7]

The good news is that teen abuse of prescription opioids remains low. The troubling trend, however, is that 70 percent of teenagers who do use opioids for nonmedical purposes combine those medications with other drugs and/or alcohol, which puts them at a higher risk of overdose.[8]

## The Legalization of Marijuana

According to a 2017 Gallup Poll, 64 percent of Americans support legalizing marijuana for recreational use. Two primary reasons for this record-high level of support are the changing perceptions regarding the relative harm to users and the windfall of tax revenue that would fill state coffers.[9]

By the end of 2017, eight states and the District of Columbia had legalized marijuana for recreational purposes. Another 21 states had passed laws legalizing the use of marijuana in some broad form, most often for medicinal purposes. More states are in the legalization pipeline as well.[10]

These three trends are creating the perfect storm through which you must help your children navigate. It is a daunting task that will require your best parenting skills and wisdom. If you feel a little pressure, don't worry. It's normal. There is a lot to learn and apply, but you can do this. You can educate, guide, and inspire your children, giving them the best possible chance to break free from these strong forces that threaten to run their lives aground.

## Clarifying Definitions

Now, I want to clarify and define some terms that will keep our discussion on track and out of the ditch. First, the topic of "drugs and alcohol" can be misleading. When we see "drugs and alcohol" written together, it is easy to assume that they are two separate things. There are drugs, and then there is alcohol. The truth is, alcohol *is* a drug. It's just one that has been prevalent and culturally acceptable in our society for a longer period than others. So to reflect this truth and to simplify our discussion, I am going to refer to both as "substances." I define a substance as any type of intoxicant, such as alcohol, marijuana, nicotine, caffeine, opiates, narcotics, or hallucinogens.[11] It is important to note that some substances are classified as legal, while others are illegal. This distinction will be important to keep in mind as we move forward in the chapter. If a substance is illegal, the conversations with your kids are going to be straightforward: It is against the law. Using them is not only detrimental to their health and wellbeing, but by using them, they risk being suspended from school and going to jail. In contrast, the sticky challenge for most parents is helping their children know how to deal with those substances that are readily accessible *and legal* at a specified age.

This definition will also be helpful when we turn to Scripture for enduring principles that can speak truth into this troubling situation. The Bible speaks only of the use of one drug—alcohol. Use of other drugs is not mentioned. Our best option is to let the biblical teachings on alcohol use speak into the broader context of intoxicants in our modern day.

In addition, I want to identify a spectrum of substance "use" that I believe will help us identify the goals we want to set as we prepare our children for a healthy future. The following four points describe this spectrum.

### Nonuse

Nonuse is refraining from the use of any substance without a prescription, legal or illegal. People abstain from substance use for a myriad of reasons—age appropriateness, accessibility, legal restrictions, religious commitments, or health concerns. This is the only approach that is free from any health risk.

### Responsible Use

Responsible use is use of a legal substance in a way that enhances one's emotional and relational sense of well-being. Also, it does not (1) impair one's abilities to carry out ordinary life roles and maintain healthy relationships, 2) occupy one's attention, time, or resources to the detriment of other life values, or (3) acutely threaten one's health. It is important to note that responsible use of any substance still involves some level of risk.

### Abuse

Abuse is use that leads to failure to fulfill major life roles and obligations at home, work, or school; involvement in activities that are physically hazardous (such as driving while intoxicated); ongoing relational and social distress; cravings for the substance to the point of giving up other previously valued activities; and inordinate amounts of time and resources spent thinking about and procuring the substance.

### Addiction

Addiction is a pattern of use that leads to the symptoms described above as abuse plus a growing tolerance of the substance, which requires more to get the same desired physiological response. Addiction also includes an increasing loss of control over the decision to use.[12]

When you consider this continuum, it becomes clear that loving and involved parents will want to guide and lead their children to nonuse or responsible use and away from abuse and addiction. The challenge, though, is discerning how to lead kids to the healthy places and away from the harmful ones. We will get to that soon enough, but first, let's add the wisdom of Scripture to the mix before we start considering solution strategies.

## Biblical Guidance

You may be surprised to learn that the biblical text speaks to each point on this modern-day spectrum of substance use. You won't be surprised, though, to find that it affirms nonuse and responsible use in different circumstances and strongly warns against a pattern of abuse and addiction. In the following section, I will point out key texts and principles regarding alcohol that can guide your conversations with your children and provide you a springboard for your own continued research.

### Substance Nonuse

The Bible does not unequivocally default to nonuse of substances, but it does provide a few compelling arguments for avoiding substances in specific instances. In the Old Testament, some individuals took what is called a Nazarite vow. The stipulations of the vow can be found in Numbers 6:2-21. During the period of the vow, an individual abstained from wine and other strong drink, cutting one's hair, and any contact with the dead. The purpose of the vow was to consecrate one's self to God by renouncing sin and devoting one's self to living a holy life.

The vow was usually taken for 30 days or 100 days at the most. Only Samson (Judges 13:4-5), Samuel (1 Samuel 1:11), and John the Baptist (Luke 1:15) are mentioned as Nazarites for life. Nonuse in the Old Testament was temporary and for a season of heightened spiritual awareness.

Moving to the New Testament, the apostle Paul challenges Christ's followers to consider their responsibility to be good self-leaders and to care for the well-being of their bodies. In 1 Corinthians 6:12-20, while specifically discussing sexual ethics, Paul concludes his thoughts by appealing to a broad principle that can be applied to a myriad of issues.

> Don't you realize that your body is the temple of the Holy Spirit, who lives in you and was given to you by God? You do not belong to yourself, for God bought you with a high price. So you must honor God with your body (1 Corinthians 12:19-20 NLT).

Paul points out to believers the spiritual reality that in view of the cost of our salvation, we no longer own our bodies. We simply are managing them for God and are responsible to him for their well-being. Therefore, when the use or misuse of any substance damages the health of our body, we dishonor the Lord's body, not just our own. Paul is asserting that the impact of the use of any substance on our bodily health is an important consideration in our decisions whether to use and to what extent.

Another argument for nonuse of substances can be made from Paul's discussion of "disputable matters" in Romans 14:1-23. Issues that were not essential to an individual's salvation kept popping up in the early church, generating misunderstandings and, at times, intense conflict. The most heated issue seemed to be whether believers could consume meat or wine purchased in the marketplace that had been offered to idols in pagan worship services. Some, who knew there were no other gods, had no issue with it. Others, who had a strong Jewish heritage, could not get over the fact that the meat and wine had been defiled. So Paul reminds believers that while they may be free in Christ to partake of that which has been sacrificed to idols, if it causes others who are fragile in their faith to stumble, then out of love, they should refrain. He concludes in verse 21, "It is better not to eat meat or drink wine or do anything else if it might cause another believer to stumble" (NLT). Here again, nonuse is not the default standard for the believer, but a loving choice one makes in certain settings and situations to ensure the growth and well-being of other believers.[13]

One other biblical teaching could make the use of substances off-limits, and that is their legal standing under the law. In Romans 13:1, the apostle Paul is clear that "everyone must submit to governing authorities" (NLT). This spiritual principle has been an effective tool in helping parents postpone their children's participation in substance use until they are of legal age and better equipped to make responsible decisions.

### Responsible Use

Responsible use of alcohol is the assumed position of both the Old and New Testaments. Wine was the common drink for the Israelites in the Old Testament and even played a major role in their worship life (Exodus 29:40; Leviticus 23:13). In Psalm 104, the psalmist describes the glory and beauty of God's creation. In his list of God's handiwork, he includes these words:

> He makes grass grow for the cattle, and plants for people to cultivate—bringing forth food from the earth: wine that gladdens human hearts, oil to make their faces shine, and bread that sustains their hearts (Psalm 104:14-15).

Wine is considered a gift from God, and its benefit for humankind is more than just the taste. It can gladden, or alter the mood of, the one partaking in a positive way. In the beginning, when God pronounced that all of creation was very good, according to the psalmist at least, wine was in the mix.

The New Testament offers an even clearer indication that responsible use is the standard expectation. In 1 Timothy 3, the apostle Paul lays out the qualifications for the two offices of the church—elders and deacons. Elders are not to be "given to drunkenness" (1 Timothy 3:3), and deacons are not to be "indulging in much wine" (1 Timothy

3:8). Responsible use, not nonuse, is the teaching and practice of the early New Testament church for its highest-level leaders.

We recognize and respect that some Christian individuals and denominations hold to a position of total abstinence from alcohol, but we maintain that this view is based on the culture rather than the Bible, especially considering the above texts. In certain instances, a good case can be made for refraining from alcohol use based on wisdom, but Scripture does not support a blanket prohibition.

### Abuse

Both testaments warn against the abuse of alcohol. The writer of Proverbs uncannily reflects our definition of abuse above.

> Who has anguish? Who has sorrow?
>> Who is always fighting? Who is always complaining?
>> Who has unnecessary bruises? Who has bloodshot
>> eyes?
> It is the one who spends long hours in the taverns,
>> trying out new drinks (Proverbs 23:29-30 NLT).

Responsible use turns into abuse when we start saying and doing things we later regret. Abuse leads to irritability and instability, which impacts everyone around us. And usually the consequences have a negative impact on the quality of our lives.

Likewise, Paul, in his letter to the Christians in Ephesus, encourages them, "Do not get drunk on wine, which leads to debauchery. Instead, be filled with the Spirit" (Ephesians 5:18). Make no mistake—our spiritual lives will also be impacted when we cross the line of responsible use and move into abuse. Like many other parts of creation, what was given as a blessing can become a curse.

### Addiction

Addiction is a complex psychological and physiological condition that was not understood in biblical times as it is today. However, biblical writers do seem to recognize the symptoms of addiction and its debilitating impact on the physical, emotional, relational, and spiritual lives of its victims. Once again, a writer of Proverbs offers a strong warning.

> Don't gaze at the wine, seeing how red it is,
>     how it sparkles in the cup, how smoothly it goes down.
> For in the end it bites like a poisonous snake;
>     it stings like a viper.
> You will see hallucinations,
>     and you will say crazy things.
> You will stagger like a sailor tossed at sea,
>     clinging to a swaying mast.
> And you will say, "They hit me, but I didn't feel it.
>     I didn't even know it when they beat me up.
> When will I wake up
>     so I can look for another drink?" (Proverbs 23:31-35 NLT).

The clearest word we have about establishing strong boundaries when it comes to substance use is found, once again, in Paul's writing to the believers in Corinth. In 1 Corinthians 6:12, he writes, "You say, 'I am allowed to do anything'—but not everything is good for you. And even though 'I am allowed to do anything,' I must not become a slave to anything" (NLT). This verse has an interesting background. Scholars tell us that the phrase "I am allowed to do anything" is a Corinthian slogan. Members of the church were taking license with grace and asserting that since they were no longer under the Jewish law, they were free to do anything they desired. Paul offered a correction to that axiom, saying a believer should refrain from anything that begins to create an addictive pattern.

Now that we have identified the most acute problems, the different ways our kids may respond to substance use, and the wisdom of Scripture, I want to turn our attention to some practical strategies and action steps that will help us lead our children to make the wise choices of nonuse or responsible use of substances.

## A Strategic Approach

As a father, pastor, and realist, I'd like to prescribe a strategic approach that lays out two goals. If you work toward these goals with reasonable success, you will prepare your children to make wise choices and avoid the heartache and tragedy of substance abuse.

- Teach and guide your children to be nonusers while they are at home under your care.
- Help your children understand what responsible use entails before they leave home for college or to enter the workforce.

As you begin to work toward these goals, you'll quickly see that just telling your kids certain things about drugs and alcohol isn't enough. You'll also need to have numerous vulnerable conversations about underlying values and meanings. You'll also need to model responsible choices in your own life. Now let's turn our attention to the conversations that will help you attain these goals.

*Empower your children to be nonusers while they are at home under your care.*

This may seem like a daunting task, but I have good news for you. As a parent, you possess the strongest influence on the decisions your children will make. According to the Substance Abuse and Mental Health Services Administration, "Most teens who do not use alcohol, tobacco, or illegal drugs credit their parents as a major factor in that decision."[14]

There are a couple of caveats, though, of which you need to be aware. Your most significant influence will be in their preteen years, and you will be most effective before they begin to use alcohol or drugs. So getting ahead of this dangerous curve is vital.[15]

For this reason, I encourage you to focus on the preteen years. In this season of parenting, you can establish three foundational values that will serve you and your kids well. The earlier you communicate these values the better. And if you lay them out effectively, you will be able to build on them as your conversations expand and mature through the years. Three values don't sound like a lot, but when placed end to end, they cover a lot of parenting ground.

## Commit to protecting and caring for them.

First, frame the boundaries and rules you set for your kids with your commitment to protect and care for them. You might say it like this: "Because I love you and care about your safety, I am going to set some rules that will protect you." These words are chosen carefully and communicate some essential truths that will build trust between you and your child for the long term. I encourage you to use this kind of phrasing when establishing any boundary. When it comes to crossing the street, you might say, "Because I love you and care for your safety, you must always look both ways before you cross the street." When your kids get a little rambunctious, you can say, "Because I love you and care for your safety, you can't slide down the banister!" This phrase will be a constant reminder of your love for them and the "why" behind the boundary you are about to set. You want them to know you are always working to keep them safe and to protect them, not simply trying to be a killjoy.

As kids begin to venture out into the wilds of the neighborhood, school, extracurricular activities, and the internet, they soon discover that there are bullies, strangers, and new experiences that can disturb and distress them. Consistently communicating and demonstrating that you are committed to their protection meets their emotional need for a sense of security, which is one of the primary emotional needs that must be met if they are going to grow into healthy and whole people. When children make this connection, they are more likely to accept your boundaries and guidelines because you are helping them feel secure.

When they are in their early elementary years and the prospect of hearing about drugs from friends or the media increases, you can set a very important early boundary: "Because I love you and care about your safety, you are not to drink alcohol or take drugs while you are under our care." The earlier you can establish this as a family rule and continually reinforce it, the greater the likelihood that your children will not fall into substance abuse in their teen or young adult years.[16]

## Focus on the importance of choices.

Second, God made everything good, but people turn good things into bad things that harm themselves and other people. This principle helps your child begin to understand that most things in life are morally neutral and that it is *how we use things*—in what spirit and for what purpose—that makes them right or wrong. The apostle Paul's word to Titus can be our guide here: "Everything is pure to those whose hearts are pure. But nothing is pure to those who are corrupt and unbelieving, because their minds and consciences are corrupted" (Titus 1:15 NLT). There will be many applications for this principle through the years as you talk through various issues with your kids, including money, sports, music, media, sex, and the internet. But for our present discussion, it will help you communicate more effectively in two areas—why some drugs are permissible while others are not, and why you or other adults can drink alcohol while your children can't.

As you begin to talk about drugs, your kids may struggle to understand why taking some drugs is okay while taking others is not okay. You will want to reassure them that the medicine the doctor prescribes is being used for the good purpose of helping them get well. On the other hand, you will want to warn them that taking drugs from people who aren't doctors can be very dangerous because they do not understand or care how bad those substances can be for them. As your kids get older and more mature, you can fill in the message with additional details—that prescription drugs from a doctor can be abused, for instance—but you want to establish early on that drugs can be a good thing when given and used the right way or a bad thing if given and used the wrong way.

Establishing this value will also be helpful should you choose to drink in your home or socially while not allowing your children to. Not surprisingly, this will be confusing to them at first. You will want to carefully explain to them that alcohol can be a good gift from God (per Psalm 104), but it is easily misused and abused and has been a destructive force in many lives. Psychologists, physicians, and lawmakers have determined that kids struggle to make wise decisions about the use of alcohol. Therefore, most states prohibit drinking under age 21 to minimize people turning something that can be considered good into something that is harmful and destructive. As your kids grow into adolescence, you will probably need to regularly reaffirm for them that while they are living at home under your care, the rule still stands. If they resist, you can remind them that when they come of age, they will be prepared to make their own decisions.

At this point it would be wise to stop and consider for a moment how your own relationship with alcohol, tobacco, or any other substance will impact your child's perception during the preteen phase. If you are a nonuser of any substance during these crucial formative years, you will have the highest level of credibility with your children. You are setting a boundary for them that you have set and abide by yourself. This approach creates the best environment for your kids to choose to be a nonuser in their teen years and beyond.[17]

If, on the other hand, you currently use a substance of any kind, you should be prepared to justify to your kids why it's okay for you and not for them. Most often, explanations will follow one of two lines—that some substances are for adults only because they are mature enough to make wise decisions about using them. or that it's against the law until people reach the legal age. No matter how eloquent you may be, though, the bottom line is that any explanation ultimately communicates, "Do as I say, not as I do." As you might expect, this parenting strategy has a rocky record of success. If your strong desire is for your kids to refrain from using substances while they are under your care and perhaps for life, you might consider abstaining from them yourself during this season of parenting. Think of it like you are taking the Nazarite vow for effective parenting!

## Emphasize making life better, not worse.

The third foundational value to communicate to your child is this: Put things in your body only if they will make your life better, not worse. This value is nothing more than a positive paraphrase of 1 Corinthians 6:12 on a kid's level: "You say, 'I am allowed to do anything'—but not everything is good for you. And even though 'I am allowed to do anything,' I must not become a slave to anything" (NLT). It is simple enough for an elementary-aged child to grasp and yet profound enough to change the life of any adult if he or she chooses to apply it. I daresay if you plant this value in your child's mind and spirit and nurture it until its roots grow deeply into his soul, you will give him an enduring inner strength that will empower him to make wise decisions in the face of even the toughest temptations.

Think of the statement from Corinthians as a template you can expand on with each new conversation with your child. As she gets closer to her middle school and high school years, you can clarify what might be included in the "things" she puts in her body. Every time something substance-related happens at her school, affects one of her friends, or pops up in the news, you have an opportunity to talk about that "thing," whatever it may be—alcohol, tobacco, marijuana, steroids, and so on—in the light of this principle.

As your kids mature and develop, you can explore in greater detail how things they ingest can make their lives worse. They need to know that the earlier a person begins drinking alcohol or using drugs, the more their brain chemistry will be altered and the higher the probability that they will succumb one day to abuse and addiction. The use of any substance has risks, and they need to be aware that if they use them, and certainly if they abuse them, they are endangering their mental and physical health. You can talk with them about their friends who become irritated and irrational when they are intoxicated. Or you can help them think through the consequences of being caught and how they will be disqualified from playing their favorite sports, expelled from school, or be in trouble with the law.

Rudolf Dreikurs is credited with the observation that "children are keen observers but poor interpreters" of the reality around them.[18] That is, kids can take in inordinate amounts of raw data about life daily, but not until their early twenties will they be able to process and comprehend the implications of what they experience. That's why using this simple biblical framework as a guide for your conversations will help you fulfill one of your most important parental roles—helping your children learn how to make wise decisions so they can grow into healthy and whole adults who fulfill God's purpose for their lives.

In the 1980s, Nancy Reagan helped launch "Just Say No," a national media campaign intended to stem the tide of recreational drug use by children and teens. It stated and reinforced a positive message, but its effectiveness was limited because it had no roots. It did not offer its intended audience a meaningful "why." Thus it could not stand against the rising current of adolescent curiosity, peer pressure, and the emotional rush or relief that drugs and alcohol initially bring.

That is why I challenge you to focus on laying, reinforcing, and building on a biblical foundation of moral reasoning. If you do, it will shape the way your children view healthy boundaries, help them understand why certain behaviors are right or wrong, and give them a filter through which they can process the crucial life choices they will face. To the degree you intentionally and consistently teach and live out these values with your children, you will give them the motivation and the tools they need to say no to substance use in their teen years.[19]

*Help your children to understand what responsible use entails before they leave home.*

Earlier, I identified myself as a father, a pastor, and a realist. As a father, my desire was that my sons would be nonusers of substances. I'm risk averse when it comes to my kids, and I like eliminating nonessential risks wherever possible! As a Christ-follower and pastor, my concern was not only for their safety but also for their spiritual health and wholeness. I would hate for substance abuse or addiction to hinder any of them from experiencing the good and beautiful lives God intends for them.

But as a realist, in view of the statistics that say 81 percent of college students have tried alcohol in their lifetimes, I would be guilty of parental malpractice if I did not at least talk to them about responsible use after age 21.[20]

Speaking of malpractice, when it comes to preparing your kids to make wise and responsible decisions about substance use, research reveals that two types of parents have a poor track record—those who are permissive and those who are overly harsh and restrictive.[21] Without any boundaries, kids are free to look for greener grass. They are susceptible to cultural trends and the influence of peers and friends, and a lack of parental protection or preparation leaves them exposed and vulnerable. Unaware and ill-equipped, many will succumb to the potent and addictive powers of drugs and alcohol.

On the other hand, some parents build a fence so high and demonize the grass on the other side so completely that they unwittingly create a seductive curiosity about the thing that is forbidden. Then when their kids are no longer under their authoritarian thumb and living in an oppressive environment, they are more likely to run right to whatever has been most stridently prohibited. The outcome of this dynamic is entirely predictable. When they turn to alcohol and drugs, these kids are unaware of their potency and ill-prepared to handle them responsibly.[22] To avoid these scenarios, consider these action steps that can encourage responsible use.

## Address responsible substance use objectively, not emotionally.

The place to begin is by being honest with your children about the possibility of responsible use. I grew up in a conservative Baptist church that drew a hard line against alcohol use. The notion of responsible use was never considered or offered as an option. On one occasion the church adopted a resolution that "any use of alcohol is abuse of alcohol." I can appreciate its compassion for those who fall victim to alcoholism, but this view makes Jesus a substance abuser, and its zeal overshoots the mark of truth. For example, 78 percent of people who take their first drink will not become alcohol dependent.[23]

When we make extreme, unfounded assertions about alcohol or other drugs, or we simply withhold the truth, we take a huge risk in losing our credibility in the eyes of our children. This is especially true when they move out and enter a more culturally diverse setting like college or the workplace. There, they will discover different perspectives, some of which will be supported more by evidence than emotion. When they do, we endanger our opportunity to continue to influence them in a positive way—and not just in the realm of substance use but in broader issues of faith as well. So being knowledgeable and truthful about the facts becomes increasingly important.

Nowhere is this truthful and straightforward approach going to be more important than in the discussions we have with our kids about marijuana use. If the current trend continues, we can expect to see the broad legalization of recreational marijuana use in the United States over the next decade. This new reality has already created a dilemma for concerned parents, pastors, and educators in states where it has been legalized. In the past, when speaking with youth about drug use, we could put marijuana on the "do not use" list because it was illegal. But now, if you live in a state where marijuana is legal, this justification is moot when your child comes of legal age. So how do we discourage our children from using marijuana? The natural recourse is to highlight the negative effects it has on those who use it.

I encourage you to go online and learn how substances such as marijuana potentially alter the wiring of one's brain, impair reaction times, and present a risk to one's ongoing physical or emotional health. As you do, identify sources that clearly have an ax to grind and a position to defend. Put those aside. Look for articles written by researchers at major universities you trust. That's where you'll find the most objective resources. This will be particularly important if you drink alcohol, as there is good reason to expect a conversation at some point with your teenager or early twentysomething child about comparing the negative effects of alcohol and marijuana. Preparing yourself for this conversation will enable you to carry on an honest, informed, and calm conversation with your children that will enhance your credibility rather than damage it.

Here's a summary of what you are going to find when you begin your research. In current scientific literature, both drinking alcohol and ingesting marijuana have elevated health risks, especially regarding the effects on the brain, memory, susceptibility to mental illness, and motor impairment. Comparatively, however, alcohol is demonstrably more dangerous. As Aaron E. Carroll, professor of pediatrics at Indiana University School of Medicine (and a father), writes,

> When my oldest child heads off to college in the not-too-distant future, this is what I will think of: Every year more than 1,800 college students die from alcohol-related accidents. About 600,000 are injured while under alcohol's influence, almost 700,000 are assaulted, and almost 100,000 are sexually assaulted. About 400,000 have unprotected sex, and 100,000 are too drunk to know if they consented. The numbers for pot aren't even in the same league.

Carroll goes on to note that 20 percent of people who drink will eventually develop a dependence on alcohol, while only 9 percent of those who use marijuana will develop a pattern of dependence. And both alcohol and marijuana impair the ability to drive safely, but the effect of alcohol on driving is significantly higher.[24]

Please do not think I share these statistics to advocate pot smoking.

I am simply trying to point out that concerned parents, especially those who may use alcohol responsibly, may face some challenging conversations with their college-aged and young adult children. From their perspective, it is disingenuous for their parents to continue to drink while forbidding their marijuana use. More and more parents may find themselves reluctantly agreeing with Professor Carroll's conclusion:

> When someone asks me whether I'd rather my children use pot or alcohol, after sifting through all the studies and all the data, I still say "neither." Usually, I say it more than once. But if I'm forced to make a choice, the answer is "marijuana."[25]

I must confess that as a young parent, I did not see these kinds of conversations coming. But now, having raised three sons, one who is a nonuser and two who drink responsibly, I am more convinced than ever that having many open, honest, and dispassionate dialogues is essential to preparing kids to make wise decisions and maintaining any kind of influence in their lives.

## Consider appropriate reasons for using substances.

At this point, one of the underlying values we laid out earlier comes into play. If substances are morally neutral, what reasons might there be for indulging in them?

Genesis 1:31 is helpful to us as we seek to answer these questions. Upon completing his work of creation, God stops and for a moment reflects on what he has made. Then he concludes, "It was very good!" (NLT) The word "good" refers to that which benefits and is useful and helpful for making someone or something better. It also has an aesthetic nuance in the original language, meaning pleasing, lovely, or beautiful.[26] With this blessing and affirmation in the background, you and your soon-to-be adult children can talk about these three reasons often used to justify the good use of substances.

*1. The enjoyment of a beverage.* A hearty ale, a robust red wine, a crisp white, and a clarifying sip of scotch are all drinks that people around the world have enjoyed for centuries. They drink them because they taste good, they highlight the taste of a gourmet meal, they slake the thirst after an afternoon of yard work, or they enhance an evening at the ballpark. When responsibly enjoyed in this way, they can be viewed as an expression of God's good gifts given in creation. The apostle Paul echoes a similar sentiment in 1 Timothy 6:17 when he says that God gives us everything for our enjoyment. I take Paul literally here. Every part of God's creation, when used in the right way and for the right reason, can be good and bring us delight.

*2. Relational connection.* Relational connection happens when people get together to share a drink. Thus Starbucks! Many of us tend to be uncomfortable in social settings, especially when we don't know everyone. And most men aren't wired to just sit around and visit. They need to be doing something for conversation to flow. Therefore, having something to drink or to hold in our hands helps us relax and sets us at ease.

I have witnessed this kind of connection firsthand. From the beginning, the men in our church enjoyed deep and authentic relationships. I attribute this to some "unofficial" gatherings that a group of our men put together. They were called "Puff and Pours." Guys would sit around a fire pit, maybe smoke a cigar or sip on a beer, and talk about their lives. If the invitation had gone out, "Hey, wanna come over and chat with some other guys?" no one would have come. Call it a "Puff and Pour," and they show up in droves.

Here's the interesting thing: No one drank too much. No one became alcohol dependent because of the gatherings. Some men drank nonalcoholic drinks. No one judged the others. But plenty of men got to know each other better, vulnerably talked about their faith journeys, and left thinking more highly of God than they did before they came. Borrowing from the words of the writer of Genesis, substance use in these gatherings can be very good when genuine connection is taking place.

*3. Joyful celebration.* Celebration is the overflowing of thankfulness for the good gifts God gives. We can celebrate privately, but it's way more satisfying to celebrate in community with others around a shared special occasion. Birthdays, graduations, weddings, promotions, and retirements are just a few of the moments that bring out special libations. The clearest biblical example of this is found in John's Gospel when Jesus performed his first miracle. Mary, trying to help a friend avert a wedding faux pas, pressed him into helping cover for the host family, who had underestimated the amount of wine needed for the weeklong celebration. Jesus was not sparing in his response. He turned water in six stone pots into 908 bottles of wine.[27] Based on this story, it is no stretch to conclude that Jesus affirms that wine can be a good and pleasing way to celebrate a joyful occasion.

### Identify and set healthy boundaries.

The apostle Paul's wisdom from 1 Corinthians 6:12 that we "must not become a slave to anything" will be the guiding principle for this final step in preparing your kids to make wise decisions on their own. To be a slave to something means you have lost your right—or in the case of substances, the ability—to choose the course or the steps of your life.

Substance dependence happens incrementally, not instantaneously. The desire for things that please and satisfy becomes, in a sense, cancerous. Desire goes rogue in our hearts and minds and begins to take over more and more of our lives. Thought, time, attention, relationships, and money gradually succumb to the will of our unintended master. How then can we help our kids set healthy boundaries should they choose to be responsible users? Here are three practical action points you can encourage them to carry out.

*1. Help your kids preset personal guidelines.* The cerebral cortex of the brain of a teenager or young adult has not fully developed the capacity to connect the dots between his decisions and long-term consequences. Rare is the teenager who goes online to discover what responsible use might entail. Alcohol distributors aren't much help either. While 9 out of 10 advertisements for alcoholic beverages advocate responsible use, none of them defines what it would look like.[28] This is where thoughtful parents come in. Helping your children think through good boundaries before they find themselves in a drinking environment may be one of the best gifts you can give them.

Here are some basic guidelines from an alcohol awareness group that will help kids avoid regrets for what they might say or do while drinking.

- No more than one drink in an hour. This will usually ensure that you remain in control of your thoughts and decisions and avoid getting drunk. If you are a male, no more than 21 drinks per week—two to three per day. If you are a female, no more than 14 drinks per week—one or two per day.

- Eat food while you drink. High-protein foods, such as cheese and nuts, slow the absorption of alcohol into the circulatory system.

- Cultivate taste by choosing quality over quantity. Learn the names of fine wines, beers, and other types of beverages. Learn what drink goes with what foods.

- Sip and skip. Drink slowly, pace yourself, and enjoy the flavors of the drink. Have a nonalcoholic drink between alcoholic ones to keep your blood alcohol down.

- Never accept a drink from someone you don't know. You can't be sure what's in it, whether alcohol or another drug intended to incapacitate you.

- Plan ahead for transportation. Don't drive when you've been drinking or ride with anyone else who has. Identify a designated driver or pay for a ride home.[29]

These suggestions may seem simple and obvious, but it would be a mistake to assume that they are in the forefront of your young adult children's minds when they go hang out with friends. Talking about them and reinforcing them before your child leaves home will give them some tools to use when navigating a new social scene.

If you are a parent of a student or young adult in a state where marijuana is legal, you will face a similar but more difficult challenge. Because marijuana does not have the social acceptability of alcohol, it may be more of a struggle for you to face up to the fact that your child is dealing with this issue and may even be using. It will be tempting to put your head in the sand and hope the issue will ultimately go away rather than setting preemptive guidelines with your child. If you do nothing, though, your children will be at the mercy of people and influences that do not have their best interests at heart. Therefore, it is imperative that you do the research, educate yourself, and in calm, two-way conversations, talk with them about what responsible use looks like. You can help them set limits on their use that keep them safer and the dialogue open so you can continue to be an influential voice in their lives.[30]

*2. Introduce the idea of intentional fasting.* Addie Zierman, in an essay in *Christianity Today*, reflects on her journey with alcohol. Having abstained as a youth, she tells of her pleasant discovery of wine as a young adult and how she is learning to drink responsibly. She recounts a memorable conversation with a friend who declined her offer of a glass of wine at dinner. Her friend noted that she was in a period of abstinence. Whenever "she feels like she's veering away from moderation she takes a month to reset. Going a month without wine helps her remember that she doesn't need it, recalibrates her mind and heart, and reminds her that she is the boss of her desires."[31]

Remind your children that God did not equip us with visible gauges that sound an alarm to let us know when we move from responsible use to abuse. It is an incremental shift that happens quietly below the surface of our consciousness. That is why intentional and responsible users of legal substances often voluntarily fast from use for a month or even longer to exercise control over the substance. During the fast, they can reflect on the level of desire that pulls them toward use. Introducing this practice to your kids as they approach legal age can give them a helpful tool to self-regulate their responsible use.

3. *Encourage your kids to establish an accountability partner.* It is no news that one of the most important elements in any recovery program for substance abuse is having a sponsor or accountability partner. Having someone to turn to in times of temptation, struggle, or failure is crucial in the journey to sobriety. We might then ask, why wait until one slips into abuse to apply this powerful principle? Encourage your children to find a friend or friends in high school, college, or the workforce who will partner with them to hold them accountable to their goals and aspirations. This can be a game changer. There will be a strong current of influence pulling your children into the party scene. Standing alone against those temptations is a herculean task. The biblical writer says it best: "A person standing alone can be attacked and defeated, but two can stand back-to-back and conquer. Three are even better, for a triple-braided cord is not easily broken" (Ecclesiastes 4:12 NLT).

## Concluding Thoughts

The longer you parent, the more you realize how many factors shape your children's lives. Their genetic footprints, the relational health of your family, the accessibility of substances, the influence of friends and peers, and the cultural influence of the media are all in the mix, along with their own character-determining choices. As you reflect on these elements, you may notice that when you begin the parenting journey, you have a lot of control over them. Then it dawns on you that as they grow older, you have less and less control over them. Before you know it, all sense of control will be diminished, and the only thing you will have left is your influence.

The key to parenting through the tough stuff, such as alcohol and drug use, is controlling the things you can, the best you can, while you can (this period begins at birth and declines in earnest with the acquisition of a driver's license). Then as your parental currency transitions to influence, you seek to influence your kids where you can, the best you can, for as long as you can (this period begins with the advent of secondary school and can last a lifetime). We could write entire chapters on each of the factors above and how your control and influence could play out in a healthy and positive way. The focus of this chapter, though, has been on the biblical values and messages you can make sure your kids hear and learn at an early age. When you consistently and graciously reinforce these values not only verbally but with your own life, you will be the strongest voice in the formation of your children's sense of moral reasoning and character. And by doing so, you will give them the navigational tools they will need to chart their way safely through the troubled waters of drugs and alcohol.

..................................................................................................

*Dear Lord,*

*As I think about the prevalence of drugs and alcohol in our society, I confess that I am concerned for my children—even afraid. There is so much at stake. I need your wisdom to guide me and your presence to be with me as I lead my children in the way that leads to life and not death. Please speak first to me about my own use of these substances. May my life and practice be a winsome example for my children. And as Jesus taught us to pray, "Lead us not into temptation, but deliver us from the evil one" (Matthew 6:13).*

*Amen.*

## Breaking It Down for Every Age

Developing a healthy relationship with drugs, tobacco, and alcohol is a process that begins well before the advent of adulthood. As a parent, the way you model the use of these substances may well be your children's first and greatest point of influence. Here are a few things to keep in mind as you help your children navigate this challenging topic through the various stages of their development.

### Elementary-Aged Kids

During the elementary years, parents still possess a tremendous amount of control over a child's environment and choices. This is an ideal time to begin having intentional conversations about the way your family chooses to use or abstain from legal substances. As outlined in this chapter, talk about the difference between drugs that are prescribed by a doctor and drugs that are purchased illegally. Talk about the laws surrounding the use of alcohol and tobacco and the reasons such laws are good and necessary. If your family chooses to abstain, help your child understand why without demonizing such substances. If your family chooses to partake, help your child understand the guardrails you've set in place to help guide and maintain responsible use.

### Tweens

During your child's tween years, your parenting dial will gradually turn from control to influence. As you continue the conversation about drugs and alcohol during this important season in your child's life, remember to speak the truth objectively rather than emotionally. Talk to your tween about the importance of healthy choices, giving him a vision for putting in his body only those things that will make his life better. Remember that your actions in this area will speak louder than your words, so carefully consider your own relationship with alcohol, drugs, and tobacco. Are there any boundaries you need to establish or strengthen in your life as you model the responsible use of these substances?

## Teens

As your teen prepares to spread her wings for independence and adulthood, talk to her about setting personal guidelines for the responsible use of legal substances. Talk about some of the appropriate reasons for responsible use, as outlined in this chapter. If applicable, share your own personal guidelines and the appropriate reasons you choose to partake of alcohol or tobacco. Talk about the role that intentional fasting can play in helping regulate responsible use, and discuss the importance of establishing accountable relationships. As you discuss these topics, keep in mind that the more you can share honestly with your teen out of your own experience, the greater the potential impact.

## Questions for Personal Reflection or Group Discussion

1. What is your personal stance and practice regarding substance use? How did you develop it? How do you think it will affect your children's view of substance use?
2. How have you developed a sense of trust and security with your children when setting boundaries for them?
3. How much do you think your kids currently know about drug and alcohol use? Where and from whom did they learn this information?
4. How much do you know about your kids' friends and their family backgrounds? What are some next steps you could take to learn more about them?
5. What else do you need to do to prepare for a knowledgeable and nonemotional conversation with your kids about drugs and alcohol?

## Additional Resources

The most up-to-date resources typically are online, where statistics and studies can be easily updated. The following government resources are particularly helpful.

### For Parents

"Boundaries with Teens" (http://www.boundariesbooks.com/articles/boundaries-with-kids/alcohol-and-drugs-boundaries-with-teens/)

*Buzzed* by Cynthia Kuhn, Scott Swartzwelder, Wilkie Wilson, and the Duke University School of Medicine. This is a great source for the straight facts about the most used and abused drugs.

Drug Abuse Resistance Education (https://www.dare.org)

National Institute on Alcohol Abuse and Alcoholism (https://pubs.niaaa.nih.gov)

National Institute on Drug Abuse (https://drugabuse.gov)

Substance Abuse and Mental Health Administration (https://www.samhsa.gov)

### For Teens

For relevant and accessible information about alcohol use, go to The Cool Spot (https://www.thecoolspot.gov).

*Alcohol Information for Teens* by Joyce Brennfleck Shannon

*Teens Talk About Alcohol and Alcoholism*, edited by Paul Dolmetsch and Gail Mauricette

# 11

# Suicide

## Paul Basden

At 16, Nina Langton's life was filled with promise. She had what every good teenager wanted—good friends, a good family, and a good school. But that facade fell apart later that year when she sank into depression, attempted suicide, and ended up in a rehabilitation facility. While she was going through rehab, her therapist helped her identify the issue that had led to her depression—she didn't like the way her body looked. Nina reflects, "I was spending a lot of time stalking models on Instagram, and I worried a lot about how I looked." She didn't know that constant comparison of her normal body with those of perfectly airbrushed models would lead to envy, self-loathing, and depression. In such a state of mind, she tried to take her life. Looking back a year later, she said, "I didn't totally want to be gone. I just wanted help and didn't know how else to get it."[1]

Nina is not alone. In 2017, the CDC released findings indicating "suicide among teen girls has reached a 40-year high."[2] It's not just 16-year-old girls either. Teenage children all over America are attempting suicide or seriously considering it. Most of these students are not what educators call "troubled kids." Like Nina, they are "good kids." A generation ago, suicide would likely not have been on their radar.

But kids in today's generation are different. They are drowning in a suicide tsunami. And the sooner we understand what's causing it, how to prevent it, and how to address it with our children, the higher the odds that they will find a sustaining reason to live.

## Grasping the Gravity of the Situation

Before looking at how to approach the topic of suicide with your kids, we first need to grasp the gravity of the situation. Here are three foundational issues that every parent must comprehend.

### The Statistics

Worldwide, almost 800,000 people die of suicide annually, which equals a person every 40 seconds.[3] On a global scale, self-inflicted death takes more lives than "war, murder, and natural disaster combined."[4] Among 15- to 29-year-olds around the world, it is the second leading cause of death.[5]

In America, more than 44,000 Americans die by suicide annually, which equates to 121 per day, or 1 every 12 minutes.[6] It is the tenth leading cause of death in the United States for all ages, occurring twice as often as homicides.[7] Suicide is the third-leading cause of death for 10- to 14-year-olds and the second-leading cause of death for 15- to 34-year-olds. For the last age group, only accidental death takes more lives.[8]

To further understand these statistics and the conversation that follows in this chapter, it will be helpful to differentiate three phrases. The terms below are typically seen as steps along the path leading to suicide.[9]

- *Suicidal ideation.* A person ponders suicide, can't stop thinking about it, and plans it.

- *Suicide attempt.* A person unsuccessfully tries to take his or her life. Statistically, only a small percentage of teenagers who attempt suicide succeed. According to Connie Goldsmith, author of *Understanding Suicide: A National Epidemic*, "For every teen who dies by suicide, at least 25 attempt it."[10]
- *Suicide.* A person succeeds in taking his or her life by means of fatal self-injury.

### The Risk Factors

When teen suicide is viewed as a social behavior, it becomes clear that several factors put some teens at higher risk than others. Here are five risk factors that every parent should know about.[11]

- *Gender.* Girls ideate and attempt suicide twice as often as boys, but boys die by suicide three times more often than girls. Still, the suicide rate among girls tripled from 1999 to 2014.
- *Race/ethnicity.* The highest rate of suicide for American teens is among whites, and the lowest rate is among blacks / African Americans.
- *Culture.* Rural teens end their lives twice as frequently as urban teens.
- *Geography.* The ten states with the highest suicide rates are all located in the West and Southwest (not including California, Washington, and Texas).
- *Accessibility.* Suicide happens far more frequently when teens have easy access to deadly means, especially guns, knives, and prescription medications.

### The Myths

Suicide is such a scary subject that much misinformation gets passed along as true. Here are five common myths, corrected by the facts:[12]

| Myths | Facts |
| --- | --- |
| People who take their lives are selfish, cowardly, or attention-seeking. | People who take their lives are in extreme pain and are desperately looking for relief. |
| People who threaten to kill themselves aren't serious. | Most people who kill themselves first make a threat. That threat is a cry for help. |
| Asking people if they are considering suicide is dangerous because it increases the likelihood they will take their lives. | Raising the subject is helpful and reduces the likelihood that a person will act on his or her ideations. |
| You shouldn't try to talk people out of suicide because you can't stop them. | Most people who consider suicide don't want to follow through. Talking to them can help them rediscover hope. |
| Real Christians don't become suicidal. | Christian faith does not magically make someone immune from suicidal thoughts. |

With these foundational facts in mind, we come to the parent-child discussion.

## What Should We Tell Our Kids?

My parents never talked to me about suicide while I was growing up. I never knew anyone who took his or her life until I was a college student.

Nor did I ever talk to my children about this topic while they were growing up. We talked about sports and school—and even sex—but not suicide. Since they had never been exposed to it, I considered it a moot subject.

How the world has changed.

Today, suicide is a hot topic in news stories, movies, songs, and TV shows. Central in the national discussion is the Netflix original TV show *13 Reasons Why*. Premiering in March 2017, it is the story of a high school girl who takes her life. In its first three weeks on the air, it amassed more than 11 million tweets—more than any other show in 2017.[13] Kids are talking about the show—and about suicide—at school, on social media, and with their peers. But they may not be talking to their parents.

So the question is, what do we tell our kids about suicide? If your children are younger, you may want to substitute "taking one's life," "ending one's life," or even "wanting to hurt oneself" for "suicide." Avoid the phrase "killing oneself" with children and with survivors of suicide, regardless of age.

## Life Is Sacred

At the heart of Christian faith is the belief that God created not just the world but each human being. God uses parents as human agents to cooperate in conception and birth, but the Creator gives life. Thus it is sacred and holy, set apart for God. As one theologian has said, "Human life belongs to God. It is His loan and blessing....Therefore respect is due to it."[14] That which is precious to God—an individual's life—must be precious to us.

The sixth commandment also communicates that life is a gift from God: "You shall not murder" (Exodus 20:13). There is no commandment in the Bible forbidding suicide, but belief in the sacred nature of each person leads us to clearly tell our children to "choose life" (Deuteronomy 30:19) over death—including our own.

Sadly, suicide is sometimes glamorized in our culture. When we talk about famous people in history who took their own lives— Socrates and his hemlock, Cleopatra and her poisonous snake, or Hemingway and his shotgun—we downplay the tragedy. Or when we idolize modern suicide victims, like Kurt Cobain, Chris Cornell, and Chester Bennington, we sometimes suggest that they died noble deaths, implying that suicide can be noble today.

At the same time, there is the ongoing debate about whether suicide should be legalized for end-of-life scenarios that involve intense suffering. On this much-debated subject, I want to share the wisdom of Dr. William E. Hull, former provost at Samford University. Dr. Hull was my friend and supervisor for four years and one of the most brilliant men I ever met. All who knew him were saddened when he was diagnosed with ALS (Lou Gehrig's disease).

Predictably, Dr. Hull confronted his new reality with courage and creativity. Even as his muscles deteriorated and his body weakened, he kept writing books. He stuck to a daily regimen of writing one laborious page per day, ultimately producing six books in 48 months. One of those books was titled *The Quest for a Good Death*. Amid excruciating suffering, he scripted these words about the sacredness of life: "I prefer to die when my body is ready for this venture, indeed is begging to be relieved of its earthly duties as the bearer of my spirit. I would not coerce my body to die either earlier or later than is natural."[15]

Dr. Hull regarded life as a gift from God, not as something that belonged to him. Therefore, he could not end it prematurely or unnaturally. This is what we mean when we affirm that life is sacred.

## Life Is Challenging

Life is not all thrills and chills—there are also some spills. Teenagers don't need to be convinced of this—puberty and peer pressure have already thrown them into disequilibrium. Younger children, however, may need help with this truth. If they have lived a relatively sheltered life, they will see people as kind and animals as nice and think that everyone lives forever. You will need to explain that sometimes bad things happen, causing us to feel sad and unhappy. This is a prime opportunity for you to share some of your own sorrows with your kids in age-appropriate ways. Such transparency has the double advantage of letting them see your humanity while helping them understand their own.

As your children grow up, look for open doors to have important conversations with them about the anxiety-producing issues that accompany adolescence. Kids sometimes let down their guard at night when they are ready for bed. This can provide a golden opportunity for you to ask them questions about physical or social challenges. These problems, often painful, are buried deep in their souls and must be coaxed out. They may talk to you about anything—having acne scars on their faces, being cut from their favorite sports teams, or being left out of desirable social circles. If they learn to deal with disappointment while they are young, then later in life they will have a better chance of resisting the temptation to throw in the towel and end their lives when things don't go their way.

The night before his crucifixion, Jesus encouraged his disciples, "I have told you these things, so that in me you may have peace. In this world you will have trouble. But take heart! I have overcome the world" (John 16:33). This is the mindset we aim to build into our children.

## Suicide Can Seem like the Answer

To use a memorable phrase, "Suicide is a permanent answer to a temporary problem."

Psychologists and counselors have identified several issues that can overwhelm children and teens, leaving them hopeless. Using age-appropriate language, talk to your children about these eight personal problems they and their peers may face.

*1. Loneliness.* This is the sense that you are socially and emotionally cut off from others. You are intended for community, but you feel isolated. This is no occasional emotion—recent research reveals that 15 to 20 percent of British adults (more than 9 million people) suffer from intense loneliness. The problem is so severe that the government has appointed a Minister for Loneliness.[16] Deep lonesomeness in turn produces discouragement, self-loathing, and despair—all of which can make suicide look like an appealing way out.[17] For followers of Jesus Christ, it is important to remember that while we may feel lonely, we are never truly alone. Feelings are powerful, but God's promises are more powerful. Children need to know that God is always with them, no matter how sad they feel. Assure them of God's presence: "Never will I leave you; never will I forsake you" (Hebrews 13:5).

*2. Depression.* This comes in two forms. The first is temporary and is virtually universal—almost everyone experiences short-term melancholy at some point in life. If you lose a job, a friend, or a marriage, you end up feeling deflated. You feel "blue" for a few days or weeks, perhaps even a few months. But eventually you find your mojo again and get back to living. The second type is long term, and it can cripple the soul. You know you're living with depression when a few "blue" days turn into nonstop "dark" days.[18] The promise of life no longer looks inviting.

How do you help your child find spiritual and emotional relief when he is feeling blue or having dark days? The Bible does not magically cure depression, but certain Scriptural passages validate depression as well as challenge it. My favorite is Psalm 42. It's the most hopeful and encouraging passage I turn to when I'm feeling down or deflated. The psalmist begs God to bless him as in the "good old days," when he felt God's presence 24/7 (verses 1-2,4). He grumbles that he has been so sad for so long, his only sustenance is his tears (verse 3). Finally he answers his complaint with confidence: "Why, my soul, are you downcast? Why so disturbed within me? Put your hope in God, for I will yet praise him, my Savior and my God" (verse 5). This psalm is life-giving and filled with hope. I suggest reading it with your kids.

*3. Anxiety.* This has been called "the most common mental health disorder in the United States."[19] Anxiety now tops depression as the primary reason college students see a counselor on campus. In 2016,

62 percent of college students reported that they felt "overwhelming anxiety."[20] Because anxiety may sound less serious than depression, we can easily dismiss it. But that would be irresponsible—deep worry often leads to depression, which in turn can lead to suicide.

Nobody is exempt from anxiety. Certainly the world offers enough problems to keep us worried all day and all night. But Christians have a way to combat despair—trusting in a good God, who is their heavenly Father. In the Sermon on the Mount, Jesus asks his followers, "Why are you worrying? Don't you know that God is your heavenly Father, and he will watch out for you?" Then he points out the secret to contentment.

> So don't worry about these things, saying, "What will we eat? What will we drink? What will we wear?" These things dominate the thoughts of unbelievers, but your heavenly Father already knows all your needs. Seek the Kingdom of God above all else, and live righteously, and he will give you everything you need. So don't worry about tomorrow, for tomorrow will bring its own worries. Today's trouble is enough for today (Matthew 6:31-34 NLT).

*4. Mental illness.* Depression can be classified and treated as a mental illness. Other, sometimes more acute forms include bipolar disorder, personality disorder, and schizophrenia. Individuals with mental illnesses struggle with the demands of life. They leave a trail of broken relationships behind them. Their future looks bleak—not just to others but to them as well. Nine out of ten people who take their lives struggle with mental illness or substance abuse or both.[21] For sufferers of mental illness, the best answer is to utilize whatever treatments are available, including counseling, medication, and prayer. For caregivers, the best answer remains genuine compassion and Christlike love.[22]

*5. Substance abuse.* Abusing chemicals is rampant in our society, often fueled by the desire to escape from reality. The chemicals may help the users shift their attention away from their problems for a while, but the crash that follows can lead to crushing despair. Substance abusers have a six times greater risk of taking their lives than those who don't abuse drugs, and "people who abuse alcohol have a ten times greater risk for suicide than the general population."[23] Sadly, in recent decades, abusing chemicals has spilled into the church in record numbers. Thankfully, the church has responded with several Christ-centered recovery programs to help people who identify their "Higher Power" with the God and Father of our Lord Jesus Christ.[24] For more on how to talk to your kids about substance abuse, see chapter 10, "Drugs and Alcohol."

6. *Bullying.* "Picking on kids" has been around for a long time, but with the rise of the internet and social media, today's bullying seems more vicious than ever—and it often sends the victim into such a tailspin that the result is suicide. Once you've been bullied repeatedly, whether in person or online, you feel hated by everyone. Eventually you wonder if you shouldn't just join the crowd and hate yourself as well. And if you hate yourself, where is the motivation to go on living?

One psychologist calls bully induced suicide "bullycide" and claims that nearly half of all suicide victims were first bullied.[25] What a tragedy! Parents must stand up and teach their kids that bullying others is off-limits. Anyone who follows Jesus is under orders to "love your neighbor as yourself."[26] This must translate to a zero-tolerance policy for bullying of any kind. At the same time, if your child is the one being bullied, tell him or her not to respond with a similar anger or it will fuel the fire. Then go with your child to speak to those who can help end the situation, including the parents of the bully, coaches, teachers, or principals.

7. *Issues related to gender identity and same-sex attraction.* Statistically, those who identify with the LGBTQ community are at higher risk for taking their lives than those who don't.[27] Bullying is often the culprit. Once again, it's up to parents to train children to use

their words to heal, not destroy. Remind them of the New Testament admonition: "Don't use foul or abusive language. Let everything you say be good and helpful, so that your words will be an encouragement to those who hear them" (Ephesians 4:29 NLT).

8. *The pitfalls and perils of social media.* Because of 24/7 access to the goings-on of everyone in their networks, teens "are relentlessly comparing themselves with their peers"—and too often concluding that they are losers.[28] One author points out the destructive impact of social media on girls:

> Studies indicate that social media can intensify depression and suicidal behavior, especially among girls. The more we submerge ourselves in the faux-reality of carefully crafted posts and curated photographs, the greater our risk of depression and suicide due to social isolation and social comparison.[29]

Something is going on in the minds of young people who are addicted to smartphones and social media, and it can be fatal. To understand this phenomenon better, we need to understand our youngest generation. Jean M. Twenge has conducted extensive research on what she terms the "iGen" generation—those born between 1995 and 2012, who have been "shaped by the smartphone and…the rise of social media." Based on her studies, she warns that this generation is "on the brink of the worst mental-health crisis in decades," caused more by smartphones than we might imagine. Surveys for the past 25 years show an unmistakable trend.

> Teens who spend more time than average on screen activities are more likely to be unhappy, and those who spend more time than average on nonscreen activities are more likely to be happy. There's not a single exception…The more time teens spend looking at screens, the more likely they are to report symptoms of depression.[30]

The conclusion is hard to deny: Addiction to smartphones and social media leads many teens down the dark road of despair and some ultimately to suicide.

This hyperconnected generation is "always on." Kids born into and raised in a digital culture do not view social media and the internet as means of information or communication but as reality—how things really are. For them, it is the world in which they live, not a window into an alternate world. The line between reality and virtual reality has blurred so much, it's now nonexistent. We are witnessing the first generation to be born into a world of internet, social media, and smartphones. They live their lives online.

Since today's children and teens have never known anything different, it will be a challenge for parents to help them see the deceptive dangers of being "always on." Perhaps Jesus's ingenious words were meant for such a time as this: "Be wise as serpents and innocent as doves" (Matthew 10:16 NRSV). Teach your kids that smartphones and social media are both a blessing and a curse. Challenge your children to consider not only the positive ways social media can be utilized, such as connecting to friends and family, but also the negative impact it can have, including unhealthy and unrealistic comparisons, internet opinions, social stigmas, cyberbullying, depression, and suicidal ideation.

These eight factors can lead children and teens to feel overwhelmed in life. Each factor taken alone may not feel soul-crushing, but if these experiences pile up one on top of another, beware of a sinking depression that can rapidly lead to despair. If despair leads to hopelessness, suicide can become an option. Talk to your kids about these factors that can build and ultimately overwhelm some people, and explain this is what makes some think that ending their lives is the best alternative. It's a faulty belief, of course. That's why your children need to know how to recognize the problems that make suicide seem reasonable in a desperate moment.

## "Make It Stop!"

Sarah Griffith Lund poignantly reminds us, "Suicide is not the result of a person choosing to die. Suicide, as one survivor shared, is an attempt to 'make the pain stop.'"[31] Frederick Buechner, renowned author and veteran minister, was ten years old when he found his father dead in the garage after inhaling car exhaust fumes. Looking back at the tragedy years later, he concluded, "When pain, horror, and despair reach a certain point, suicide is perhaps less a voluntary act than a reflex action."[32] Taking one's life becomes the ultimate escape from pressures and problems that never seem to go away.[33] Seen from this perspective, suicide is a misguided act of self-protection that tragically ends in self-destruction.

Are there other reasons that people end their lives? Probably so. One psychologist offers four reasons people attempt suicide:

- They are attempting to manipulate someone who is emotionally close to them.
- They see it as an opportunity to get revenge on someone who has hurt them.
- They are making an unconscious cry for help.
- They want to escape the crushing burdens of life once and for all.[34]

Some combination of these factors stands behind every sad story of suicide. Yet it's hard to conclude that the ultimate cause could be anything other than utter anguish. According to a Princeton professor and Nobel prizewinner for studies in human well-being and happiness, teen suicides are "deaths of despair."[35] This is confirmed by medical studies of suicidal patients in psychiatric wards, revealing that there is only one difference between those who attempt suicide and those who don't—hope.[36]

As you're talking to your children about pain that leads to suicide, this may also be the time to talk about cutting. A phenomenon that became more prevalent on our national stage more than a decade ago, it is a red flag that a young person is experiencing deep pain and may be considering suicide.

What is cutting, and why do kids do it? Cutting is intentionally harming yourself with sharp objects like razors, knives, and scissors. It is usually done on a body part that can be covered up by clothes.

Why would anyone willfully hurt his or her own body? That's a good question with many answers. It may be a way for people to get their minds off mental suffering that is stressing them out; or a way to express, maybe even manage, their guilt, shame, or self-hatred; or a way to punish themselves for who they are or what they've done. One teen-suicide expert says that cutting is a way to avoid suicide—it's a cry for help.[37]

To protect your children from the practice of cutting, teach them two biblical truths. First, God loves them so much that he took their sin and shame upon himself through his Son, Jesus.

> For everyone has sinned; we all fall short of God's glorious standard. Yet God, in his grace, freely makes us right in his sight. He did this through Christ Jesus when he freed us from the penalty for our sins (Romans 3:23-24 NLT).

As a result, "Now there is no condemnation for those who belong to Christ Jesus" (Romans 8:1 NLT). Jesus was condemned so that we could be accepted. He paid the final sacrifice for our sins when he died in our place. There is no reason for any of us to suffer any more for our own sins. The writer of Hebrews concurs: "When sins have been forgiven, there is no need to offer any more sacrifices" (Hebrews 10:18 NLT).

Second, their bodies belong to God, and he wants them to honor them—for his sake and for theirs. The apostle Paul made this clear:

> Don't you realize that your body is the temple of the Holy Spirit, who lives in you and was given to you by God? You

do not belong to yourself, for God bought you with a high
price. So you must honor God with your body (1 Corinthians 6:19-20 NLT).

A teen who believes that her body belongs to God and that the
Spirit of God lives in her will possess valuable spiritual resources
when faced with the temptation to inflict self-harm.

## Suicide Has More Than One Victim

The person who takes his life is not the only victim—everyone he
loved or who loved him is also a victim. Al Hsu was a young newly-
wed when his mother called one day to deliver the tragic news that
his father had taken his life. Al records his unbelief, grief, and even-
tual recovery in *Grieving a Suicide: A Loved One's Search for Comfort,
Answers, and Hope.*[38] The title suggests what suicide survivors know:
Grief over a suicide is messy, complicated, and multilayered.

Let's unpack the grief process. I believe that grief is the God-given
response of our body and soul to the loss of someone or something
that has given us purpose. When we lose a job, a marriage, a parent,
or a child, we grieve—that is, we feel deep pain because we must continue to live without someone or something that made life meaningful. Death is one of the most painful losses to grieve. When death is
from natural causes, the survivors can find some relief in the mystery
found in the Old Testament: "There is a time for everything, and a
season for every activity under the heavens: a time to be born and a
time to die" (Ecclesiastes 3:1-2).

But when we lose a loved one because she took her life, the grief
process gets more complex. We still feel deep loss that leads to sadness, maybe even to depression of our own. But now we face questions we can't answer.

Did I do something to cause this?

Could I have done anything to prevent it?

How could this person do this to me?

Why was this person so selfish?

How can I ever explain this to anyone?

If he could take his life, am I capable of doing the same?

These questions plague the survivors. They haunt. They interrogate. They suffocate.

That's why suicide has more than just one victim. The survivors carry a weight that can feel unbearable. This awareness will help you talk to your children if they lose a friend or loved one to suicide. They will feel emotions they have never felt before with an intensity that may stun them. You can help them understand that it's normal to feel everything from shock to anger to fear to sadness to guilt to depression.

You can also help them find comfort in the shortest verse in the Bible: "Jesus wept" (John 11:35). Not even the Son of God was above weeping over the loss of a good friend. Giving your kids permission to cry will help them embrace the complicated grief resulting from suicide and slowly work through it.[39] If your child is dealing with the death of a friend from suicide, you might also consider taking her to see a Christian counselor who can provide a safe place to process feelings that could otherwise overwhelm your child and cause addition harm.

## Suicide Is Always Tragic but Never Unforgivable

At some point in the history of the church, suicide was pronounced as the unforgivable sin. That conclusion was based on a faulty interpretation of 1 Corinthians 3:17, where the apostle Paul wrote, "God will destroy anyone who destroys this temple. For God's temple is holy, and you are that temple" (NLT). At first glance, it sounds like Paul is warning people against destroying their bodies (God's temple) because they are holy to God. But the Greek word for "you" is plural—in Texas, we would say "all y'all." So Paul is not referring to how you treat your own human body but discussing how we treat the unity of Christ's body, which is the church. He is telling those who are causing divisions in the church that they are destroying God's temple.[40] This passage has nothing to do with suicide.

Al Hsu, whose story is mentioned above, calls suicide what it is: "I put suicide in the literary category of tragedy. In Greek or Shakespearean tragedy, somebody is undone by an internal flaw, and the tragic hero dies because something has gone wrong in their story."[41] Help your child see that when someone takes his life, it is a tragic ending to his story. Earlier in my life, I called suicide a sin—and in the sense that it misses God's ideal, it is a sin. But I have found that such a statement heaps shame on the survivors and especially on the family. I now say it's a tragic ending to a story. That allows me to "weep with those who weep" without confusing their grief even more.[42]

## Suicide Can Be Prevented

Suicides are not inevitable. Despairing teens want a reason to live. Hopeless children are looking for hope. How can we equip our kids to encourage their peers who struggle with suicidal ideation or have tried to take their lives? How can parents help their kids help their friends prevent suicide?

There are several basic steps to follow in responding to anyone who shows signs of potential suicide. If your child is in middle school or high school, she can take these steps with your guidance. If your child is younger, you will need to take these steps on her behalf.

First, encourage anyone who is exhibiting suicidal symptoms to call the National Suicide Prevention Lifeline at 1-800-273-8255, available 24 hours every day. A trained responder will be ready to help him face his fears without taking his life.

Second, urge her to talk through her pain with a professional counselor. Cognitive-behavioral therapy (learning to replace toxic thoughts with healthy thoughts so that healthy behavior can replace toxic behavior) has been especially helpful in addressing suicidal ideation among teens.[43]

Third, ask him to consider joining a support group. In such a setting, the suicidal student does not feel alone—thus addressing the issue of loneliness. He also meets students who have decided to choose life rather than death and can find inspiration in their stories—thus addressing the issue of despair.

Fourth, if she has tried to take her life or is making overt threats to do so, tell her she needs the resources of an inpatient treatment center. There are two advantages to entering such a facility: First, they are safe places where children or teens cannot harm themselves. Second, they are healing places where therapists aim to help suicidal students find a reason to live.

Followers of Jesus have three other preventive resources to offer kids who are considering ending their lives.

First is corporate worship. According to a Harvard University study of suicide and religious practice among women between 1996 and 2010, "Those who attended any religious service once a week or more were five times less likely to attempt suicide. Of the 6,999 Catholic women who said they attended Mass more than once a week, none committed suicide."[44] Meeting God in worship gives spiritual purpose that strengthens us for the tests of life—including the ultimate test of deciding to live rather than take our lives. Jesus's words to his followers come into full play here: "The thief comes only to steal and kill and destroy; I have come that they may have life, and have it to the full" (John 10:10). The evil one wants to destroy the image of God in every human—Jesus came to restore it. In worship, we are reminded that life is found in Jesus only.

Second is Christian community. If suicide is caused by despair, then despair can be caused by a diminishing sense of community and belonging—what one writer calls "increased social fragmentation."[45] With virtual relationships replacing face-to-face friendships and online communication supplanting personal conversation, it is no exaggeration to say that "social bonds are weakening, and the social fabric is fraying."[46] That's why church attendance and small-group participation deter suicide. Gathering together is a social experience that provides community to counteract our loneliness. The "one another" commands in the New Testament—to love one another, pray for one another, confess our sins to one another, and dozens more—require community.

Third is compassion. Jennifer Michael Hecht has penned a book on suicide prevention titled *Stay*.[47] Hecht is not a Christian—she's an atheist who grew up Jewish. Yet her argument against suicide echoes the Golden Rule: "If suicide has a pernicious influence on others, then staying alive has the opposite influence: it helps keep people alive. By staying alive, we are contributing something precious to the world."[48] Something precious indeed—the life of someone whom God created and for whom Christ died!

If there's one takeaway for children of all ages, it is this: Treat every person you meet with dignity and kindness. This is at the heart of following Jesus, and it can prevent more suicides than we can imagine. A morality tale comes from a physician, Dr. Jerome Motto, who saw more than his fair share of patients take their lives. As a longtime psychiatrist in San Francisco, he regularly talked with patients who wanted to end it all by jumping off the Golden Gate Bridge (which happens to be the number one suicide site in America). Although he consistently counseled them not to do so, some ignored his warnings. Here is the story, as Dr. Motto tells it, of one patient who jumped to his death in the 1970s.

> I went to this guy's apartment afterward with the assistant medical examiner. The guy was in his thirties, lived alone, pretty bare apartment. He'd written a note and left it on his bureau. It said…"I'm going to walk to the bridge. If one person smiles at me on the way, I will not jump."[49]

Apparently no one smiled.

## Conclusion

What do you tell your kids about suicide? Tell them that God loves each person. Tell them that life is sacred. Tell them that people take their lives when the pain they feel is greater than the hope they can picture. Tell them that suicide can be prevented. And tell them to smile at everyone as often as they can.

........................................................................................................

*O Lord,*

*This topic frightens me. If others' children can take their lives, mine could do the same. Just thinking about it makes me sick to my stomach. I love my kids and want them to live long lives filled with purpose and meaning. I can't fathom how sad they would have to be for death to look better than life.*

*Empower me to see this epidemic as you see it, so that I may be filled with compassion for all who struggle with suicide, especially young people.*

*Open the door for me to have candid talks with my children about suicide—and push me through that door if I stand on the outside too long. Their lives are worth my next step.*

*Amen.*

## Breaking It Down for Every Age

Talking about death with a child is a daunting prospect, but knowing what to say about suicide can leave parents especially baffled. If your child is displaying signs of depression, anxiety, or suicidal ideation, we recommend that you seek immediate assistance from your pediatrician or a licensed Christian counselor. Beyond that, here are some helpful things to keep in mind as you navigate the difficult topic of suicide with your child, tween, or teen.

### Elementary-Aged Kids

In a few years, your child will enter the challenging tween stage, full of changing hormones and increased social pressures. With that in mind, take the opportunity during these foundational elementary school years to establish some protective countermeasures. Focus on making your child feel celebrated, loved, and supported, not because of what she achieves but because of who she is. Help your child learn to acknowledge, communicate, and regulate her emotions. Establish yourself as a trusted voice in your child's life. Ask questions, and really listen when your child shares her thoughts and feelings.

### Tweens

As the tween years dawn, your child's friendships will move to a new level of prominence. Keep a close eye on his interactions and involvement with social media. Ask questions about his classmates, friendships, and who he's following online. If your child seems quiet or withdrawn, don't wait for him to initiate a conversation. Knock on the door, sit down with him, and say, "You seem sad. What's going on? I'm here to listen." Don't dismiss or minimize your tween's feelings of sadness, frustration, or loneliness. Listen…and let your child know he is loved, seen, and heard.

### Teens

During the teen years, help your child prioritize worship gatherings and connecting with a community of believers, as described in this chapter. In addition to combatting the despair caused by social isolation, these habits will set your teen up for success in the years after she leaves your home. Serving others is another spiritual practice that will help your teen gain a grander vision for her life. Look for opportunities to serve together and then talk about what you learn from those shared experiences.

## Questions for Personal Reflection or Group Discussion

1. What statements would your child need to make for you to decide that a conversation about suicide would be in order?
2. What are the three things you would most want your child to hear from you?
3. List five insights from this chapter you think will enrich your conversation.
4. Do you have any concerns about your child struggling with lingering depression? If so, have you taken him to a counselor or physician to receive help? Who and what are your best available resources to help your child if he entertains suicidal thoughts or expresses suicidal intentions?

## Additional Resources

If you are interested in further reading on this subject, these resources may be helpful.

### For Parents

*Preventing Suicide: A Handbook for Pastors, Chaplains, and Pastoral Counselors* by Karen Mason

*Suicide and Mental Health* by Rudy Nydegger

*Teens and Suicide* by Cherese Cartlidge

*Understanding Suicide: A National Epidemic* by Connie Goldsmith

# Conclusion

## Paul Basden

Raising children to love Jesus in a sinful world places you, the parent, in a precarious situation. If you are a helicopter parent, placing too many limits on your kids' freedom, then they may rebel—against you, the church, and even God. If you are a free-range parent who is so laissez-faire in your discipline that your kids don't have the boundaries they need to be safe from themselves and from others, then they may miss the allure of Jesus in their formative years—and never look for him later in life.

Parenting in today's world is tough stuff indeed!

That's the reason for writing this book. We want to be on the journey with you. We hope the wrinkles on our foreheads, which we accumulated in large part through raising our kids to adulthood, have resulted in time-tested wisdom that will serve you well.

As you think back over our answers to some crucial questions, you will notice several things.

First, we intentionally addressed both theological and moral questions. We did that because we believe kids are regularly thinking about two things:

"What do I believe?"

"How should I act?"

We could have written a book about only biblical and doctrinal topics, but that would have resulted in a very different product—more of a Bible answer book.

We also could have focused only on hot-button moral issues, but that too would have created a different book, something along the lines of a dos-and-don'ts manual.

We hope our choice of theological topics (like evil and suffering) and ethical issues (like partying) will help you answer the real questions your kids are asking.

Second, we have attempted to articulate the biblical message while remaining sensitive to culture. In each chapter, we've tried to hold God's Word and our world in a healthy tension. While this is not an easy task, it's necessary. As John Stott has pointed out, preachers can fall into one of two errors:

- They preach from the Bible but fail to preach to modern culture. This is like trying to build a bridge from the world of Scripture to the world of culture but leaving the end of the bridge suspended in midair because of cultural ignorance.
- They preach to modern culture but fail to preach from the Bible. This is like trying to build a bridge from midair to modern culture but doing so with no firm foundation because of biblical ignorance.[1]

Our goal? We want to be as faithful to the Bible as we are sensitive to the modern world—and vice versa. We want to apply the biblical text to the modern context without misrepresenting either. We make no claim to have done so perfectly, but that's been our clear aim.

Third, we believe our approach can help parents and children who are devoted Christians as well as those who aren't. Believers and seekers alike can find practical truth for living in these pages. We have a simple mission statement at the church where we serve as pastors: "helping people find and follow Jesus Christ."[2] That mission has informed us at every point in this book. Our greatest joy would be to know that we have helped people come to initial faith in Jesus Christ and to grow in their faith in the Lord.

As you've noticed, each of these three concluding points reflects a "both/and" mentality, not an "either/or" mindset. In the words of James Collins and Jerry Porras, we embrace "the Genius of the AND."[3] We think we have some solid reasons for doing so:

- Jesus is *both* human *and* divine.
- Humans are *both* created in the image of God *and* tainted by evil and sin.
- Christians are *both* saved *and* sinful.[4]
- The Bible is *both* inspired by God *and* written by human authors.
- Raising kids is *both* the most enjoyable *and* the most exhausting experience in life!

If we have been able to save you from some of the pitfalls of parenting and equip you to have meaningful conversations with your kids along the way, then we will be truly thankful. With that in mind, here is our prayer for you and your family.

> In times of trouble, may the Lord answer your cry.
>     May the name of the God of Jacob keep you safe from
>     all harm...
> May he grant your heart's desires
>     and make all your plans succeed.
> May we shout for joy when we hear of your victory
>     and raise a victory banner in the name of our God.
> May the Lord answer all your prayers (Psalm 20:1,4-5
> NLT).

Amen and Amen!

# Notes

## Chapter 1: The Bible

1. Richard Lederer, "56 B.C. and All That," *National Review*, March 1, 1993, 51-52; "Question and Answer," *National Review*, December 31, 1995, 36-39.

2. Jana Duckett, "Kids Say the Darndest Things," Beliefnet, http://www.beliefnet .com/faiths/galleries/20-questions-kids-ask-about-god.aspx?p=2; Suzee Skwiot, "18 Funny Questions Kids Have Asked About God," CafeMom, May 6, 2015, http://thestir.cafemom.com/big_kid/185378/18_funny_questions_kids_have.

3. "No one can know a person's thoughts except that person's own spirit, and no one can know God's thoughts except God's own Spirit. And we have received God's Spirit (not the world's spirit), so we can know the wonderful things God has freely given us" (1 Corinthians 2:11-12 NLT).

4. See John Ortberg, *Faith and Doubt* (Grand Rapids, MI: Zondervan, 2008), 51-52.

5. Sally Lloyd-Jones, *The Jesus Storybook Bible* (Grand Rapids: ZonderKidz, 2012).

6. YouVersion's *The Bible App for Kids* is available to download for free at https://www .bible.com/kids.

7. Mark Batterson, *Circle Maker* (Grand Rapids, MI: Zondervan, 2011), 94.

## Chapter 2: Partying

1. John Eldredge, *Beautiful Outlaw* (New York, NY: FaithWords, 2011), 58.

## Chapter 3: Divorce

1. Gary Richmond, *The Divorce Decision* (Dallas, TX: Word Publishing, 1988), 127-28.

2. John Claypool, *Mending the Heart* (Cambridge, MA: Cowley, 1999), 50.

3. John Greenleaf Whittier, "Dear Lord and Father of Mankind," 1872. For additional insights into the meaning of this hymn, see the meditation "Our Ordered Lives" by Fisher Humphreys in Paul Basden, ed., *Encountering God in the Prayers of Others* (Cleveland, TN: Parson's Porch, 2014), 73-74.

## Chapter 4: Having Sex

1. Linda Klepacki, "What Your Teens Need to Know About Sex," Focus on the Family, posted 2005, http://www.focusonthefamily.com/lifechallenges/ love-and-sex/purity/what-your-teens-need-to-know-about-sex.

2. Eleanor Barkhorn, "Getting Married Later Is Great for College-Educated Women," *The Atlantic*, March 15, 2013, https://www.theatlantic.com/sexes/archive/2013/03/ getting-married-later-is-great-for-college-educated-women/274040/.

3. Tyler Charles, "(Almost) Everyone's Doing It," *Relevant Magazine*, September/October 2011.

4. Charles, "(Almost) Everyone's Doing It."

5. Lauren Winner, *Real Sex: The Naked Truth About Chastity* (Grand Rapids, MI: Brazos Press, 2005), 9-26.

6. Harry Emerson Fosdick, *The Manhood of the Master* (San Francisco, CA: Inkling Books, 2002), quoted in Rueben Job and Norman Shawchuck, *A Guide to Prayer* (Nashville, TN: The Upper Room, 1983), 283.

## Chapter 5: Other Religions

1. Will Herberg, *Protestant, Catholic, Jew: An Essay in American Religious Sociology* (New York, NY: Doubleday, 1955).

2. Pew Research Center, "America's Changing Religious Landscape," Religion & Public Life, May 12, 2015, http://www.pewforum.org/2015/05/12/americas-changing-religious-landscape.

3. C.S. Lewis, *Mere Christianity* (London, UK: Geoffrey Bles, 1952), 29.

4. For more information, see Sally Becker, *Sunflowers and Snipers: Saving Children in the Balkan War* (Gloucestershire, UK: History Press, 2013).

5. See Fritz Ridenour, *So What's the Difference? A Look at 20 Worldviews, Faiths, and Religions and How They Compare to Christianity* (Ventura, CA: Regal Press, 2001).

6. Lewis, *Mere Christianity*, 29.

7. Daniel Migliore, *Faith Seeking Understanding* (Grand Rapids, MI: Eerdmans, 2004), 327.

8. Antonia Blumberg, "U2's Bono Opens Up About Jesus, God and Praying with His Kids," Religion, *Huffington Post*, April 11, 2014, http://www.huffingtonpost.com/2014/04/11/bono-jesus_n_5127614.html.

9. For more detail on this passage in its context in Matthew, see pages 57–58 in chapter 3, "Divorce."

## Chapter 6: Racism

1. Manny Fernandez, Richard Perez-Pena, and Jonah Engel Bromwich, "Five Dallas Officers Were Killed as Payback, Police Chief Says," *New York Times*, July 8, 2016, https://www.nytimes.com/2016/07/09/us/dallas-police-shooting.html.

2. Spencer Perkins and Chris Rice, *More Than Healing: Racial Healing for the Sake of the Gospel* (Downers Grove, IL: InterVarsity Press, 2000), 12.

3. Christopher Ingraham, "Three Quarters of Whites Don't Have Any Non-white Friends," *Washington Post*, August 25, 2014, https://www.washingtonpost.com/news/wonk/wp/2014/08/25/three-quarters-of-whites-dont-have-any-non-white-friends/?noredirect=on&utm_term=.f75668c09b16.

## Chapter 7: Why Bad Things Happen

1. Philip Yancey, *Disappointment with God: Three Questions No One Asks Aloud* (Grand Rapids, MI: Zondervan, 1988), 181-83.

## Chapter 8: Porn

1. Melinda Tankard Reist, "Sex Before Kissing: How 15-Year-Old Girls Are Dealing With Porn-Obsessed Boys," Fight the New Drug, November 10, 2017, https://fightthenewdrug.org/sex-before-kissing-15-year-old-girls-dealing-with-boys/.

2. Peter S. Vogel, "SCOTUS: From Pornography's 'I Know It When I See It' to Social Media's 'I Don't Get It,'" *E-Commerce Times*, December 8, 2010, https://www.ecommercetimes.com/story/71402.html.

3. Wendy Maltz and Larry Maltz, *The Porn Trap: The Essential Guide to Overcoming Problems Caused by Pornography* (New York, NY: William Morrow Paperbacks, 2010), quoted in Cordelia Anderson, *The Impact of Pornography on Children, Youth, and Culture* (Holyoke: NEARI Press, 2014), 5-6.

4. Anderson, *Impact of Pornography*, 11. Anderson lists corporations that fly under the radar, including cable companies, internet providers, and software developers.

5. Educate and Empower Kids, *How to Talk to Your Kids About Pornography* (Bourne, TX: Educate and Empower Kids, 2016).

6. Anderson, *Impact of Pornography*, 7-8.

7. Educate and Empower Kids, *How to Talk to Your Kids*, 25.

8. Educate and Empower Kids, *How to Talk to Your Kids*, 24-25; Fight the New Drug, "How Porn Changes the Brain," updated August 23, 2017, https://fightthenewdrug.org/how-porn-changes-the-brain.

9. Anderson, *Impact of Pornography*, 8-9.

10. Claudine Gallacher, "Hidden Porn Exposure Leads Young Boy to Sibling Abuse," *Protect Young Minds*, September 22, 2016, https://protectyoungminds.org/2016/09/22/hidden-porn-exposure-sibling-abuse.

11. Educate and Empower Kids, *How to Talk to Your Kids*, 26-27.

12. Gail Dines, "Growing Up in a Pornified Culture," TEDx Talks, April 28, 2015, https://www.youtube.com/watch?v=_YpHNImNsx8.

13. We wrote about this briefly in chapter 4, "Having Sex." In this chapter, we will look more closely at how to tap into this power.

14. Andy Crouch, *The Tech-Wise Family* (Grand Rapids, MI: Baker Books, 2017), 140.

15. Brian X. Chen, "What's the Right Age for a Child to Get a Smartphone?" *New York Times*, July 20, 2016, https://www.nytimes.com/2016/07/21/technology/personaltech/whats-the-right-age-to-give-a-child-a-smartphone.html.

16. Jonathon van Maren, "The Horror Stories Are Real. Don't Give Your Children a Smartphone," *LifeSite News*, October 4, 2016, https://www.lifesitenews.com/blogs/the-madness-of-giving-your-child-a-smartphone.

17. Chen, "What's the Right Age."

18. Jesse Weinberger, *The Boogeyman Exists; and He's in Your Child's Back Pocket: Internet Safety Tips for Keeping Your Children Safe Online, Smartphone Safety, Social Media Safety, and Gaming Safety* (self-pub., CreateSpace, 2014). This is a comprehensive treatment of the issues we have been addressing above.

19. Kristen Jenson and Gail Poyner, *Good Pictures Bad Pictures: Porn-Proofing Today's Young Kids* (Richland, WA: Glen Cove Press, 2014).

20. Educate and Empower Kids, *How to Talk to Your Kids*, 18, 26-27.

21. Educate and Empower Kids, *How to Talk to Your Kids*, 31. What follows is a summary of the Educate and Empower Kids plan.

22. Educate and Empower Kids, *How to Talk to Your Kids*, 31.

23. Another helpful framework for kids can be found in *Good Pictures Bad Pictures*. Even though the book is for younger children, the authors' "CAN DO" pneumonic device will be helpful for older kids. See Jenson and Poyner, *Good Pictures Bad Pictures*, 31-41.

24. Harry Emerson Fosdick, *The Manhood of the Master* (San Francisco: Inkling Books, 2002), quoted in Rueben Job and Norman Shawchuck, *A Guide to Prayer* (Nashville, TN: The Upper Room, 1983), 283.

25. C.S. Lewis, *Yours, Jack: Spiritual Direction from C.S. Lewis* (Grand Rapids, MI: Zondervan, 2008), 292-93.

## Chapter 9: Same-Sex Attraction

1. "Hillary Clinton, Giuliani March in N.Y. Gay Parade," *Washington Post*, June 26, 2000, https://www.washingtonpost.com/archive/politics/2000/06/26/hillary-clinton-giuliani-march-in-ny-gay-parade/93eab33a-6e64-4c3b-9035-f8dbd1a2e30e.

2. We differentiate "homosexuality," defined as having a same-sex orientation, from "homosexual behavior," defined as engaging in same-sex erotic activity. We do not believe that homosexual orientation is condemned or even addressed in the Bible, so we do not consider it to be sinful. We do believe that homosexual behavior is addressed and considered sinful in the Bible.

3. This chapter focuses on same-sex attraction. Recently, gender identity and confusion have become hot topics. For differing perspectives on the transgender issue, see Mark Wingfield, "Seven Things I'm Learning About Transgender Persons," Opinion, *Baptist News Global*, May 13, 2016, https://baptistnews.com/article/seven-things-im-learning-about-transgender-persons/#.Wxq60UgvyUk; Walt Heyer, "Drop the T from LGBT," *The Federalist*, April 21, 2016, http://thefederalist.com/2016/04/21/drop-the-t-from-lgbt/.

4. There are five other brief passages in Scripture that may be considered. However, I have not done so because one of them reinforces what we find in these major passages (1 Timothy 1:8-11), and four of them likely refer to the ancient practice

of sexually assaulting male outsiders who were visiting the area as a sign of power and authority, not to be identified with homosexual practice as we know it today (Genesis 19:4-9; Judges 19:22-26; 2 Peter 2:1-10; Jude 3-7).

5. Tony Campolo, *20 Hot Potatoes Christians Are Afraid to Touch* (Dallas: Word Publishing, 1988), 117. Campolo has since changed his mind and considers same-sex relationships to be permissible for Christians. See Ruth Gledhill, "Tony Campolo Calls for Full Acceptance of Gay Christian Couples in the Church," *Christian Today*, June 8, 2015, christiantoday.com/article/tony.campolo.calls.for .full.acceptance.of.gay.christian.couples.in.the.church/55718.htm.

6. See Campolo, *20 Hot Potatoes*, 112-13, 116.

7. Philip Yancey, *What's So Amazing About Grace?* (Grand Rapids, MI: Zondervan, 1997), 161-75.

8. Andrew Marin, *Love Is an Orientation* (Downers Grove, IL: InterVarsity Press, 2009), 25-26.

9. John Burke, *No Perfect People Allowed* (Grand Rapids, MI: Zondervan, 2005), 163.

10. The three approaches mentioned here have been popularized by Stanley J. Grenz in *Welcoming but Not Affirming: An Evangelical Response to Homosexuality* (Louisville, KY: Westminster John Knox, 1998).

11. This third approach is the one our church (Preston Trail Community Church in Frisco, Texas) seeks to follow. For a summary of the results of a six-year study of the topic by our elders, which led us to this conclusion, as well as a video statement in response to the 2015 Supreme Court ruling on gay marriage, visit https:// prestontrail.org/gaymarriage.

## Chapter 10: Drugs and Alcohol

1. Centers for Disease Control and Prevention (CDC), "Fact Sheets—Binge Drinking," Alcohol and Public Health, last updated May 10, 2018, https://www .cdc.gov/alcohol/fact-sheets/binge-drinking.htm.

2. Substance Abuse and Mental Health Services Administration (SAMHSA), "Table 6.88B: Alcohol Use in the Past Month Among Persons Aged 18 to 22, by College Enrollment Status and Demographic Characteristics: Percentages, 2013 and 2014," *Results from the 2014 National Survey on Drug Use and Health: Detailed Tables*, https://www.samhsa.gov/data/sites/default/files/NSDUH-DetTabs2014/ NSDUH-DetTabs2014.htm#tab6-88b.

3. SAMHSA, "Table 6.89B: Binge Alcohol Use in the Past Month Among Persons Aged 18 to 22, by College Enrollment Status and Demographic Characteristics: Percentages, 2013 and 2014," *Results from the 2014 National Survey on Drug Use and Health: Detailed Tables*, https://www.samhsa.gov/data/sites/default/files/ NSDUH-DetTabs2014/NSDUH-DetTabs2014.htm#tab6-89b.

4. CDC, "Fact Sheets."

5. National Institute on Alcohol Abuse and Alcoholism (NIAAA), "Alcohol

Facts and Statistics," National Institutes of Health (NIH), updated June 2017, https://www.niaaa.nih.gov/alcohol-health/overview-alcohol-consumption/alcohol-facts-and-statistics.

6. National Institute on Drug Abuse (NIDA), "Opioid Overdose Crisis," NIH, revised March 2018, https://www.drugabuse.gov/drugs-abuse/opioids/opioid-overdose-crisis.

7. NIDA, "Overdose Death Rates," NIH, revised September 2017, https://www.drugabuse.gov/related-topics/trends-statistics/overdose-death-rates.

8. NIDA, "Teens Mix Prescription Opioids with Other Substances," NIH, updated April 2013, https://www.drugabuse.gov/related-topics/trends-statistics/infographics/teens-mix-prescription-opioids-other-substances.

9. Samuel Stebbings, Grant Suneson, and John Harrington, "Pot Initiatives: Predicting the Next 15 States to Legalize Marijuana," *USA Today*, January 5, 2018, https://www.usatoday.com/story/money/2017/11/14/pot-initiatives-predicting-next-15-states-legalize-marijuana/860502001.

10. Stebbings, Suneson, and Harrington, "Pot Initiatives."

11. Will Meek, "Substance Use, Abuse, & Addiction: The 11 Symptoms of Substance Use Disorders," *Psychology Today*, January 2, 2014, https://www.psychologytoday.com/blog/notes-self/201401/substance-use-abuse-addiction. Thanks to Dr. Meek for the definition of "substance" and for clarifying the lay of the substance abuse land. If you suspect a member of your family has a substance abuse problem, Meek's helpful guide to the severity of the symptoms of substance abuse may help you determine when you need to get professional help.

12. Meek, "Substance Use." DSM-5, the American Psychiatric Association's diagnostic manual, no longer refers to "dependence" or "addiction" but uses the phrase "substance use disorder," which denotes different levels of severity. For the purposes of this chapter, I am using the less technical and more recognizable term "addiction."

13. As a contextual reminder, the point of contention regarding wine was not that it was alcoholic but that it had been used in sacrifices offered to idols. In a similar vein, the issue of eating meat was not a question of whether someone should be a vegetarian but a question of whether it was acceptable to eat meat that had been offered to an idol. But in some places and times, drinking alcohol (including wine) can be perceived to lead someone to stumble. In that instance, refraining from use may be the most Christlike response for a believer.

14. Center for Substance Abuse Prevention (CSAP), *Keeping Youth Drug Free*, HHS Publication No. (SMA) 17-3772 (Rockville: SAMHSA, 2017), https://store.samhsa.gov/product/Keeping-Youth-Drug-Free/SMA17-3772.

15. NIAAA, "Make a Difference: Talk to Your Child About Alcohol," NIH Publication No. 16-4314, revised 2009, https://pubs.niaaa.nih.gov/publications/makeadiff_html/makediff.htm.

16. CSAP, *Keeping Youth Drug Free*, 3.

17. CSAP, *Keeping Youth Drug Free*, 31.

18. John Claypool, *Mending the Heart* (Cambridge, MA: Cowley, 1999), 50.

19. The focus of this chapter is to help walk you through the tough topic of substance use and abuse with your child from a biblical perspective. But the work of parenting also includes key decisions about how to treat and support your children as they are growing up under your care. For some excellent counsel in this regard, see CSAP's free resource *Keeping Youth Drug Free*.

20. Chris Elkins, "Alcohol Facts and Stats," DrugRehab.com, May 25, 2018, https://www.drugrehab.com/addiction/alcohol/facts-and-stats/.

21. CSAP, *Keeping Youth Drug Free*, 26.

22. For a helpful article on this dynamic, see Gwen Dewar, "Authoritarian Parenting: What Happens to the Kids?," *Parenting Science*, updated June 2017, https://www.parentingscience.com/authoritarian-parenting.html.

23. C. Lopez-Quintero, J. Pérez de los Cobos, D.S. Hasin, et al., "Probability and Predictors of Transition from First Use to Dependence on Nicotine, Alcohol, Cannabis, and Cocaine: Results of the National Epidemiologic Survey on Alcohol and Related Conditions (NESARC)," *Drug Alcohol Depend* 115, nos. 1-2 (May 1, 2011): 120-30.

24. Aaron Carroll, "Alcohol or Marijuana? A Pediatrician Faces the Question," *New York Times*, March 16, 2015, https://www.nytimes.com/2015/03/17/upshot/alcohol-or-marijuana-a-pediatrician-faces-the-question.html.

25. Carroll, "Alcohol or Marijuana?"

26. Walter Brueggemann, *Genesis, Interpretation: A Bible Commentary for Teaching and Preaching* (Atlanta, GA: John Knox Press, 1982), 37.

27. John Eldredge, *Beautiful Outlaw* (New York, NY: FaithWords, 2011), 58.

28. Margaret Raskob, "What Does the 'Please Drink Responsibly' Disclaimer Really Mean?" *The Buzz* (blog), National Center on Addiction and Substance Abuse, https://www.centeronaddiction.org/the-buzz-blog/what-does-"please-drink-responsibly"-disclaimer-really-mean.

29. Julie Hynes, "Safe Drinking Tips for Young Adults," PreventionLane, August 9, 2013, https://preventionlane.org/young-adults-alcohol-safe-drinking-tips.

30. To consider what responsible use may look like, see Stanton Peele, "The Need to Identify Sensible Marijuana Use," *Psychology Today*, January 3, 2014, https://www.psychologytoday.com/blog/addiction-in-society/201401/the-need-identify-sensible-marijuana-use.

31. Addie Zierman, "A Toast to My Journey with Wine: Calling for a More Moderate Discussion about Moderate Drinking," *Christianity Today*, March 17, 2016, https://www.christianitytoday.com/women/2016/march/toast-to-my-journey-with-wine.html.

## Chapter 11: Suicide

1. Markham Heid, "We Need to Talk About Kids and Smartphones," *Time*, December 27, 2017, https://time.com/4974863/kids-smartphones-depression/.

2. Heid, "We Need to Talk."

3. World Health Organization (WHO), "Suicide Data," Mental Health, 2018, http://www.who.int/mental_health/prevention/suicide/suicideprevent/en/.

4. Connie Goldsmith, *Understanding Suicide: A National Epidemic* (Minneapolis, MN: Twenty-First Century Books, 2017), 8.

5. WHO, "Suicide Data."

6. American Foundation for Suicide Prevention (AFSP), "Suicide Statistics," 2018, https://afsp.org/about-suicide/suicide-statistics/.

7. AFSP, "Suicide Statistics."

8. AFSP, "Suicide Statistics."

9. Goldsmith, *Understanding Suicide*, 8.

10. Goldsmith, *Understanding Suicide*, 38.

11. Cherese Cartlidge, *Teens and Suicide* (San Diego, CA: Reference Point Press, 2017), 12-18; Goldsmith, *Understanding Suicide*, 21-35.

12. Goldsmith, *Understanding Suicide*, 90-91; Cartlidge, *Teens and Suicide*, 12; Karen Mason, *Preventing Suicide: A Handbook for Pastors, Chaplains, and Pastoral Counselors* (Downers Grove, IL: InterVarsity Press, 2014), 41.

13. Elizabeth Wagmeister, "Netflix's '13 Reasons Why' Is Most Tweeted About Show of 2017," *Variety*, April 21, 2017, https://variety.com/2017/tv/news/netflix-13-reasons-why-twitter-most-popular-show-2017-1202392460/.

14. Karl Barth, *Church Dogmatics*, vol. 3, part 4 (Edinburgh: T. & T. Clark, 1961), 397.

15. William E. Hull, *The Quest for a Good Death: A Christian Guide* (Birmingham, AL: Samford University Press, 2014), 90.

16. Ashley Fetters, "What Loneliness Does to the Human Body," *New York Magazine*, January 22, 2018, https://www.thecut.com/2018/01/the-health-effects-of-loneliness.html.

17. Gary R. Collins, *Christian Counseling: A Comprehensive Guide* (Waco, TX: Word Books, 1980), 90.

18. Cartlidge, *Teens and Suicide*, 32.

19. Benoit Denizet-Lewis, "Why Are More American Teenagers Than Ever Suffering from Severe Anxiety?" *New York Times Magazine*, October 11, 2017, https://www.nytimes.com/2017/10/11/magazine/why-are-more-american-teenagers-than-ever-suffering-from-severe-anxiety.html.

20. Denizet-Lewis, "Why Are More American Teenagers."

21. Goldsmith, *Understanding Suicide*, 21.

22. Since losing her son to suicide in 2013, Kay Warren has passionately promoted care for the mentally ill. See Ed Stetzer, "Suicide, Mental Illness, and the Church: An Interview with Kay Warren," *Christianity Today*, October 2017, https://www .christianitytoday.com/edstetzer/2017/october/suicide-mental-illness-and-church -interview-with-kay-warren.html.

23. Goldsmith, *Understanding Suicide*, 37.

24. For two such programs, check out Celebrate Recovery (https://www .celebraterecovery.com) and re:generation (http://www.regenerationrecovery.org/). Celebrate Recovery also has a recovery program for teens called The Landing.

25. Rudy Nydegger, *Suicide and Mental Health* (Santa Barbara, CA: Greenwood, 2014), 10.

26. Matthew 22:39.

27. Cartlidge, *Teens and Suicide*, 31; Goldsmith, *Understanding Suicide*, 34.

28. Denizet-Lewis, "Why Are More American Teenagers."

29. Halee Gray Scott, "Messages from the Edge: Suicide Notes on Social Media," *Christianity Today*, January 2016, http://www.christianitytoday.com/women/2016/ january/messages-from-edge-suicide-notes-on-social-media.html.

30. Jean M. Twenge, "Have Smartphones Destroyed a Generation?" *The Atlantic*, November 3, 2017, https://www.theatlantic.com/magazine/archive/2017/09/ has-the-smartphone-destroyed-a-generation/534198/.

31. Sarah Griffith Lund, "10 Things We Know About Mental Illness," *Sarah Griffith Lund* (blog), September 30, 2017, https://sarahgriffithlund .com/2017/09/30/10-things-we-know-about-mental-illness/.

32. Frederick Buechner, *Whistling in the Dark: A Doubter's Dictionary* (San Francisco, CA: HarperSanFrancisco, 1988), 116.

33. Collins, *Christian Counseling*, 77.

34. Collins, *Christian Counseling*, 77.

35. Aaron Kheriaty, "Dying of Despair," *First Things*, August 2017, https://www .firstthings.com/article/2017/08/dying-of-despair.

36. Kheriaty, "Dying of Despair."

37. Goldsmith, *Understanding Suicide*, 38-44.

38. Albert Y. Hsu, *Grieving a Suicide: A Loved One's Search for Comfort, Answers, and Hope* (Downers Grove, IL: InterVarsity Press, 2002).

39. See chapter 4 in John H. Hewett, *After Suicide* (Philadelphia: Westminster, 1980) for specific suggestions about talking with your children following a suicide in the family. He is very helpful in calling parents to be honest (versus using euphemisms about suicide), to listen (versus censoring emotions that make you feel uncomfortable), to recognize how kids grieve (including guilt, denial, fear, and anger), and to know the signs of "acting out childhood grief"—including physical symptoms and illness, over-responsibility, and rebellion against authority.

40. The NIV translation clears up this issue by rendering the last part of the verse as "For God's temple is sacred, and you together are that temple."

41. Al Hsu, "The Truth about Suicide," interview by Morgan Lee, *Christianity Today*, October 20, 2017, https://www.christianitytoday.com/ct/2017/november/suicide -americans-taking-their-own-lives-church-al-hsu.html.

42. Romans 12:15 NLT.

43. Cartlidge, *Teens and Suicide*, 48-51.

44. Kheriaty, "Dying of Despair."

45. Kheriaty, "Dying of Despair."

46. Kheriaty, "Dying of Despair."

47. Jennifer Michael Hecht, *Stay: A History of Suicide and the Arguments Against It* (New Haven, CT: Yale University Press, 2013).

48. Katelyn Beaty, "Staying Alive in a Suicidal World," *Christianity Today*, August 12, 2014, http://www.christianitytoday.com/ct/2014/july-august/staying-alive-in -suicidal-world.html.

49. Tad Friend, "Jumpers: The Fatal Grandeur of the Golden Gate Bridge," *New Yorker*, October 13, 2003, https://www.newyorker.com/magazine/2003/10/13/jumpers.

## Conclusion

1. See John R. W. Stott, *Between Two Worlds: The Art of Preaching in the Twentieth Century* (Grand Rapids: Eerdmans, 1982).

2. For more information, visit prestontrail.org.

3. James Collins and Jerry Porras, *Built to Last: Successful Habits of Visionary Companies* (New York, NY: HarperCollins, 1994), 44.

4. In the words of Martin Luther, the believer is *simul justus et peccator*, "at the same time justified and a sinner."